The New
African-American
Kitchen

The Kitchen Diva!

The New African-American Kitchen

by Angela Shelf Medearis

Published by:
Lake Isle Press, Inc.
16 West 32nd Street, Suite 10-B
New York, NY 10001
(212) 273-0796
E-mail: lakeisle@earthlink.net

Distributed to the trade by:
National Book Network, Inc.
4501 Forbes Boulevard, Suite 200
Lanham, MD 20706
1(800) 462-6420
www.nbnbooks.com

Library of Congress Control Number: 2008929058

ISBN-13: 978-1-891105-39-5
ISBN-10: 1-891105-39-6

Book and cover design: Liz Trovato

Editors: Pimpila Thanaporn
        Katherine Trimble

This book is available at special sales discounts for bulk purchases as premiums or special editions, including customized covers. For more information, contact the publisher at (212) 273-0796 or by e-mail, lakeisle@earthlink.net

First edition
Printed in the United States of America

10 9 8 7 6 5 4 3 2 1

Dedicated to the wonderful women in my family, especially to the memory of my great-grandmother Angeline Wilson Carolina, my grandmothers, Willie Mae Davis and Marybelle Weathers, and my aunt Florine Davis Walker, with love and thanks.

Acknowledgments

I want to thank the Lord for the gifts of writing and cooking. He's blessed me with other gifts and talents, but I love these two the most. I'm also thankful for my mother, Angeline Shelf, and my sisters, Marcia Shelf Orlandi and Sandra Fergins, for all their years of love, friendship, and food, and for inspiring me to write my first cookbook. To my wonderful husband and favorite dinner companion, Michael, for his love, encouragement, and support, and to my favorite kitchen assistants, my daughter, Deanna, and my granddaughter, Anysa, for all of the wonderful times we've shared cooking together on Sunday afternoons. I also want to thank my friend and assistant, Dynisha Cole, for her help with all things Diva! Special thanks and love goes to Hiroko Kiiffner for her enthusiasm and support and for making the publishing process an exciting experience. I love y'all!

Contents

Introduction

The New African-American Kitchen is not only a cookbook, it's a love letter to my family, my friends, and all of the wonderful viewers who watch The Kitchen Diva! public television show. I've prepared many of the recipes contained in this cookbook on television, and I enjoy sharing my interest in culinary history with my viewers.

In 1992, my sisters, Sandra and Marcia, urged me to write a cookbook to record all of my mother, Angeline's, and my grandmother, Willie Mae Davis's, wonderful recipes. Although I had written more than fifty children's books, I'd never even thought about writing a recipe, let alone an entire cookbook. At that time, I was a passable cook, but I had a bad attitude about preparing a meal. I looked at cooking as a chore that had to be done, not as an act of love.

Once I changed my attitude, I was able to change my life and make a positive impact on the lives of others. I call my new point of view "Diva-tude." Now I love to cook, and you can taste it in every dish I prepare. One of my favorite parts of a cookbook tour is the opportunity to share a little "Diva-tude" with others. I enjoy talking with my audience about the things I've learned about history, food, recipes, business, and most importantly, what I've learned about life.

During the creation of my first cookbook, *The African-American Kitchen*, I fell in love with cooking and with culinary history. *The New African-American Kitchen* is my opportunity to write about all of the fascinating history and food trends I've discovered since I struggled to write and publish my first cookbook more than fifteen years ago.

The New African-American Kitchen contains some of the recipes that form the basis of the cultural cooking heritage of many African-Americans. It is filled with authentic and historic recipes from West Africa, the West Indies, and Central America. It contains recipes from the U.S. South that were called "receipts" by slave cooks and their masters, and recipes that are a spicy blend of African, Latino, West Indian, European, and American foods. It also has a chapter with information about living a healthier life, as well as recipes for those who struggle with diet-related illnesses such as diabetes and heart disease.

This cookbook has been lovingly infused with all of the things I've learned since I first began wearing a feather boa and a red satin apron to do cooking demonstrations on television as a guest chef and cookbook author in 1994. Things have changed in American kitchens since the Kitchen Diva first appeared on camera. We've enthusiastically embraced herbs, spices, meats, and produce that were considered exotic only a few decades ago. We've also learned the many ways that our culinary history and our diets impact our health.

In 2004, the Lord blessed my husband, Michael, and I to transform our company, Diva Productions, Inc., into a multimedia company. We've created a number of television projects for children based on our children's books, produced radio and television programs, and animated DVD projects. In 2007, we began producing The Kitchen Diva! show for public television stations nationwide.

During each program, I teach tasty ways to feed a family on a budget by using a combination of locally grown, organic, and commercially prepared foods, including vegetarian recipes and alternative sources of protein. One thing I've learned during my short tenure on television: If you're an African-American woman who wants folks to try tofu, it helps if you're wearing what I often wear on the show—a feather boa and a red satin apron with the hot pads in the bustier. I had often spoken about food and health issues dressed in traditional business garb. Then the Kitchen Diva was born and demanded that the masses and the media pay attention to her message. If you're trying to convince die-hard pork fat lovers to taste a vegetarian entrée, a red feather boa trumps a tailored business suit every time.

I know that some people stop to watch The Kitchen Diva! because they can't believe that an African-American woman is cooking on television. Even though historically, African and African-American cooks and chefs have made significant contributions to the cuisines of the world, we're invisible in the media. I'm not only making great meals on The Kitchen Diva!, I'm also making history.

Television is a forum for me to teach families about history, health, and nutrition while encouraging them to support the farmers and the markets in their areas. It gives me great joy to display and make use of the beautiful produce I've purchased at my local farmer's market. I've become an expert at sharing fascinating tidbits of culinary history while I slice and dice ingredients on camera.

There is a miraculous feeling that abides when family and friends gather together to share a wonderful meal; there is comfort in the ways of old, and joy in learning something new. The contents of this cookbook are my culinary legacy; now they are yours as well.

Remember to put a lot of love in your cooking!

—Angela Shelf Medearis
The Kitchen Diva!
Austin, Texas
2008

The Roots of Soul Cooking
Africa

The man that eats no pepper is weak; pepper is the staff of life.

—Yoruba proverb

The African Kitchen

My African ancestors left me a number of intangible heirlooms: a will to survive, a strong sense of family, a love of foods that connect me to the past, and a desire to preserve and to pass on my history. The more I studied culinary history, the more I wanted to know about what African-Americans traditionally eat and why we prepare our food the way we do. Along this journey I found ingredients, seasonings, and methods of preparation that linked the captive slave cooks from Africa to the Caribbean Islands and to North and South America. Just as countless cultures have introduced the foods of their homeland to America, African-Americans have a cuisine that is rooted in Africa.

I also wanted to use this cookbook to examine the effect slavery had on the food, culture, and cooking techniques in the places where Africans were held captive. African slave chefs created one of the first "fusion" cuisines in America. They creatively combined foods similar to those they prepared in Africa with the culinary traditions of the places where they were enslaved. These inventive cooks deserve much more credit than historians have given them for what are now considered standard preparation techniques and traditional recipes.

Historical African, South American, Caribbean, and West Indian recipes form the heart of this book. The "receipts" from American slave cooks form its soul. Ancient and modern, traditional and nontraditional cooking, celebrations, and holidays are combined to create the recipes in the African-American and the Healthy Living chapters. Each chapter is the beloved offspring of the preceding one, but all have roots in Africa.

My African ancestors are an invisible but strong presence in my kitchen. Part of their legacy to me and to America can be found in a simmering pot of spicy okra gumbo, in a delicious handful of peanuts, in a steaming bowl of black-eyed peas and rice on a cold New Year's Day, and in freshly baked rolls, warm from the oven and covered with sesame seeds (which are called benne in some African dialects) and the oil they produce. The African names for these foods are still used today.

My first experience with African food occurred when a friend from Ghana lived with my family. Having graciously offered to prepare a traditional African dinner, she served us a tomato-based stew called palaver, which is also known as palava in different African regions. The stew contained small portions of beef and spinach served over rice (see recipe, page 36). It had a wonderful aroma, and we couldn't wait to try it. She warned us that it was hot; we thought it would be like the spicy Mexican dishes we're used to eating. Several glasses of cold water later, we realized that we were wrong! It was one of the hottest dishes any of us had ever attempted to eat. I found out later that the word palaver, which originated in West Africa, means "trouble."

Peppers give African dishes their distinctive flavor. The rule of thumb seems to be that the hotter the climate in Africa, the hotter the foods. A study conducted in 1954 found that eating the hotter kinds of peppers in warm climates causes a reaction called gustatory sweating. Gustatory sweating has a cooling effect on the body and is stimulated only by hot foods. Research indicates that the hotter the foods, the cooler the body.

I've learned to love African cooking. I've also learned to adjust the heat. The African recipes in this chapter use varying amounts of fresh and commercially prepared peppers. Some specify red peppers, others green chiles. Recipes that call for red peppers refer to the half-inch-long, fiery-hot red cayenne peppers. Recipes that call for green chiles refer to the mild five- to six-inch-long California or Anaheim chiles or, for those who prefer hotter dishes, the green, two- to three-inch-long jalapeño chiles. These chiles can be found in most grocery stores dried, ground, canned, or fresh; you can use them in these recipes in any of these forms.

Remember always to wear gloves when preparing fresh peppers. Failure to do so will result in a burning sensation in your hands and any other part of your body you touch. Never use hot water to rinse dried or fresh peppers; it may send up fumes that will irritate your eyes and nose. You can crush dried peppers in a mortar and measure them out in this form.

When preparing fresh peppers, it's best to remove the stems and seeds with your gloved fingers. However, you can use a paring knife if the ribs of the pepper are thick and fleshy. Removing the seeds doesn't affect the flavor but greatly decreases the heat. Always wash your hands thoroughly with soap and cold water when you have finished preparing peppers. Be sure to clean any utensils or surfaces you have used.

African Culinary History

Africans were captured or sold into slavery by the millions. Most of the captives came from the coasts of West, East, and South Africa, as well as a few countries in the continent's interior. Their harrowing journey from Africa to North, Central, and South America and the West Indies was known as the Middle Passage.

Stripped of every possession but their memories and their spirit, they struggled to survive on the slave ships. The last remnant of home on these treacherous journeys came via the meals they received from their captors: John Barbot, a slave merchant, stated that "a ship that takes in 500 slaves, must provide above 100,000 yams." This formula provides about 200 yams per person for the harrowing, months-long trip across the waters from Africa to America.

Alexander Falconbridge, an English doctor who made several voyages on board slave ships, describes a typical meal in his 1788 narrative, *Account of the Slave Trade on the Coast of Africa*:

"The diet of the Negroes while on board, consists chiefly of horsebeans [fava beans] boiled to the consistence of a pulp; of boiled yams and rice and sometimes of a small quality of beef or pork. They [the sailors] sometimes make use of a sauce composed of palm-oil mixed with flour, water and red peppers, which the sailors call slabber-sauce. Yams are the favorite food of the Eboe or Bright Negroes, and rice or corn of those from the Gold and Windward Coasts; each preferring the produce of their native soil."

The cargo holds of the slave ships brought crops directly from Africa for the captives to eat during their passage to the New World. These crops included legumes and produce that were the main components of the African diet, including rice, peanuts, okra, millet, sorghum, guinea melon, black-eyed peas, licorice, cassava, yams, watermelon, sesame seeds (also known as benne), and kidney and lima beans.

The seedlings for these and other crops were often transported from Africa on the slave ships. The African captives knew how to make the plants grow and how to cook and season the produce. These ingredients became the mainstays of Southern cuisine as the African captives became the cooks in their master's kitchens and incorporated the foods that were transported on slave ships into the daily meals they prepared. African plants were cultivated by the slaves on farms and plantations and in the small gardens they were sometimes allowed to tend for their own use. The success of the early South Carolina rice crops was due in large part to the knowledge African slaves had about the planting and cultivation of the grain.

The captives were severed forever from their homes and from their old ways of life. They were given new names, forced to learn a new language and to labor under conditions that would have destroyed weaker spirits. They found few comforts in this strange new land. In their scant moments of privacy, they continued their African traditions—in language, music, religious customs, and food. Finding foods similar to those in Africa and preparing them as they had been prepared in their homeland was a consolation to the captives, evoking warm memories of family, ceremonies, and feast days.

The impact of slavery changed the face of the New World. To erroneously limit African and African-American culinary contributions to Southern regional recipes is a disservice to the millions of unsung African and African-American cooks who created classical dishes using ingredients in innovative ways that are still celebrated today all over the United States.

Spiced Oil and Sauces

Niter Kebbeh (Spiced Clarified Butter)

YIELD: 2 CUPS

This spicy clarified butter is used by Ethiopian cooks to add flavor to their food. Niter kebbeh is often used when preparing doro we't (page 35).

1 pound (4 sticks) unsalted butter
3 tablespoons chopped garlic
1 small onion, chopped
1 (1- to 2-inch) piece ginger, peeled and
  crushed

1/4 teaspoon cardamom pods, crushed
1/8 teaspoon ground nutmeg
11/2 teaspoons ground turmeric
1 teaspoon ground cloves
1 cinnamon stick

1. Cut the butter into small pieces. Place the pieces in a heavy 4-quart saucepan; melt the butter over high heat until foamy. Be careful not to burn it. Stir in the garlic, onion, ginger, cardamom, nutmeg, turmeric, cloves, and cinnamon stick. Reduce the heat to low, but do not cover the pan. Simmer the mixture 45 minutes, stirring frequently.

2. Pour the mixture into a jar through a sieve lined with several layers of cheesecloth. Strain the oil repeatedly until it is clear in order to remove any spices or solids; leaving any pieces in the butter will turn the oil rancid. Cover the oil and store it in the refrigerator for up to 6 months.

African Carrot Sambal

YIELD: 6 SERVINGS

This condiment has a sweet and spicy flavor that goes well with a bowl of black beans.

8 medium carrots, coarsely grated
2 teaspoons salt
1 large green bell pepper, seeded and
    diced

1 small onion, minced
1/4 cup red wine vinegar
1/2 teaspoon cayenne pepper, or to taste
1 teaspoon sugar

1. In a bowl, combine the carrots and salt. Let stand at room temperature about 30 minutes to extract the excess moisture from the carrots. Squeeze the carrots between paper towels and drain any liquid from the bowl.

2. In a separate bowl, stir together the bell pepper, onion, vinegar, cayenne pepper, and sugar until the sugar is completely dissolved. Add the carrots and gently blend. Let the mixture marinate at room temperature 15 minutes before serving.

Ata Sauce (Pepper Sauce)

YIELD: 1 CUP

Ata is the Yoruba word for chile pepper. This sauce, excellent on baked or broiled meats, puts bottled American hot sauces to shame.

2 cups diced red bell pepper
1 large onion, diced
2 large tomatoes, sliced

1/2 teaspoon to 2 tablespoons crushed red
    pepper flakes, to taste
1/4 teaspoon salt
1/2 cup peanut oil

1. Put the bell pepper, onion, tomatoes, red pepper flakes, and salt in a blender and pulse until coarsely chopped. In a heavy frying pan, heat the oil over medium-high heat until hot but not smoking; sauté the mixture until the pepper is tender and the onion is golden brown. Simmer uncovered over low heat 10 minutes, stirring occasionally.

2. Place the pepper sauce in a container, cover it tightly, and refrigerate it. The sauce may be refrigerated for up to 1 week. The oil may separate, so stir well before using the sauce.

Berber and Tainey Sauce

YIELD: 1 1/2 CUPS

This flavorful sauce is named for the North African Berber tribes famous for their tradition of horsemanship. Use the sauce to marinate or baste chicken and barbecued meats, or serve it as a condiment at the table.

1/4 cup raisins
1/4 cup fresh lemon juice
5 tablespoons butter, softened
2/3 cup peanut oil
3 teaspoons honey
1 tablespoon smooth peanut butter

1/2 teaspoon curry powder
1/4 teaspoon crushed red pepper flakes
1/4 teaspoon dried basil
1/4 teaspoon dried marjoram
1/4 teaspoon ground allspice
Pinch chopped fresh mint

1. In a medium bowl, soak the raisins in the lemon juice 15 minutes, or until plump. Add the butter, peanut oil, honey, peanut butter, curry powder, red pepper flakes, basil, marjoram, allspice, and mint. Combine the ingredients well, cover, and refrigerate. The sauce may be refrigerated for up to a week. The oil may separate, so stir well before using the sauce.

East African Banana Jam

YIELD: ABOUT 3 CUPS

This jam is wonderful with bread or as a cake filling. Aluminum utensils react with the lemon juice and bananas giving them a metallic taste as well as discoloring them, so use stainless steel, wooden, plastic, or enamel utensils when preparing this dish.

6 ripe bananas

2 cups sugar

1/2 cup fresh lemon juice

1 tablespoon grated lemon zest

1. Slice the bananas into 1/4-inch rounds. In a large nonreactive bowl, stir together the sugar, lemon juice, and lemon zest until the sugar dissolves. Fold in the banana slices until evenly coated. Cover the bowl with plastic wrap or foil and let the bananas marinate at room temperature for at least 1 hour.

2. Put the bananas and marinade in a saucepan. Bring the mixture to a boil, stirring frequently. Reduce the heat to low and simmer, uncovered, 30 minutes, stirring occasionally. The jam should be thick enough to mold with a spoon. Immediately ladle the jam into an airtight container and refrigerate. East African Banana Jam will keep for 2 to 3 days.

Appetizers

Akara Balls (Bean Scoops)

YIELD: 4 SERVINGS

I love making akara balls or kosai as they're called in some parts of Africa. The traditional recipe calls for removing the skins from the black-eyed peas by soaking them overnight and then rubbing the peas between the palms of your hands and rinsing them repeatedly to remove the skin. Soaking the peas overnight makes them tender. Akara taste great hot or cold.

1 1/2 cups dried black-eyed peas, soaked overnight and the skins removed
1/2 cup warm water
1 egg
1/2 teaspoon chili powder

1/2 teaspoon salt
1/2 teaspoon black pepper
1 cup chopped onion
2 cups vegetable oil

1. In a blender, grind the peas 3 minutes. Gradually add the water, grinding until the mixture turns into a paste. Scrape the bean paste into a bowl and whisk 5 minutes to aerate the mixture. Add the egg, chili powder, salt, and black pepper and beat again until the mixture is smooth. Add the onion and combine, stirring until the mixture is smooth.

2. In a deep-fryer or a deep skillet, heat the oil over medium-high heat until hot but not smoking. Deep-fry tablespoonsful of the bean mixture, a few at a time, until golden brown. Drain the akara balls on paper towels.

VARIATIONS:
Akara awon: Mix in 1/2 cup finely minced okra along with the onion.
Akara meatballs: Add a second egg and 1 pound lean ground beef to the bean mixture.

Ghana Kelewele (Plantain Appetizer)

YIELD: 6 SERVINGS

This appetizer is easy to prepare and makes a wonderful snack. In Ghana, kelewele is also served for breakfast and as a side dish, much like french fries.

2 cups cooking oil

2 tablespoons water

1 teaspoon ground ginger

1/2 teaspoon salt

1/2 teaspoon cayenne pepper

6 large unripened plantains, peeled and sliced 1/2 inch thick

1. In a deep-fryer or a skillet deep enough to cover the plantain slices, heat the oil over high heat until hot but not smoking.

2. In a small bowl, combine the water, ginger, salt, and cayenne pepper. Drop the plantain slices into the bowl 1 by 1, coating each piece evenly.

3. Deep-fry the plantain slices until golden brown. Drain on paper towels.

Nigerian Eggplant Appetizer

YIELD: 4 SERVINGS

The eggplant and sesame seeds in this recipe make an unusual and nutritious dip for raw vegetables.

1 large eggplant, peeled and sliced

1 teaspoon sesame seeds

1 clove garlic

1/2 teaspoon salt

1/4 cup fresh lemon juice

2 tablespoons chopped parsley

1. Preheat the oven to 350 degrees. Place the eggplant slices on a cookie sheet and bake the eggplant until tender, about 10 minutes, or microwave, uncovered, 5 to 7 minutes. In a blender, grind the sesame seeds and garlic into a paste. Add the eggplant and blend until smooth. Blend in the salt and lemon juice. Mound the dip on a shallow dish and sprinkle with the chopped parsley.

South African Pickled Fish

YIELD: 4 SERVINGS

This wonderful South African dish must "pickle" for two days before it's ready to be served.

1/4 cup vegetable oil
6 to 8 halibut fillets (2 pounds total), each about 1/2 inch thick

MARINADE:
1/4 cup vegetable oil
3 large onions, sliced 1/8 inch thick
1/2 cup packed light brown sugar
3 tablespoons chopped hot green chiles

1 tablespoon curry powder
1 tablespoon ground ginger
2 large bay leaves, crumbled, plus 2 whole bay leaves
1 teaspoon ground coriander
2 teaspoons salt
2 cups malt vinegar
1 cup water

1. In a heavy skillet over moderate heat, heat 1/4 cup vegetable oil until hot but not smoking. Rinse the fillets in cool water and pat dry. Fry the fillets in the oil until golden brown, about 5 minutes on each side. Drain the fillets on paper towels until cool.

2. To prepare marinade: Discard the oil remaining in the skillet and wipe the skillet dry with paper towels. Heat 1/4 cup oil over medium-high heat until hot but not smoking. Add the onions and cook, stirring frequently, until they are golden brown. Add the sugar, chiles, curry powder, ginger, crumbled bay leaves, coriander, and salt. Cook over low heat 2 minutes, stirring frequently. Slowly stir in the vinegar and water and bring the mixture to a boil over high heat; reduce the heat to low and simmer the marinade, uncovered, 10 minutes.

3. Remove any bones and skin from the fillets and discard; cut the fish into 2-inch squares. Spread about a third of the halibut evenly in a 9x12-inch glass or enameled serving dish. Cover the halibut with 1 cup or so of the marinade, then add another layer of halibut, alternating the fish and marinade. Lay the whole bay leaves on top and cover the dish tightly with plastic wrap. Refrigerate 2 days before serving.

Peanuts Piri-Piri

YIELD: 8 SERVINGS

It has been hard to determine exactly where the name piri-piri—or pili-pili, as it is known in some parts of Africa—originated. Some say it is a Portuguese word for the small red malagueta pepper. Others say it is a West African name for a small red peppercorn common to that region. In Mozambique, piri-piri is the name of the sauce used to coat nuts, beans, or plantains and has become a national dish known for its spiciness.

2 tablespoons vegetable oil
1 clove garlic, mashed
1/2 to 2 tablespoons cayenne pepper,
   to taste

1 teaspoon chili powder
1 pound shelled peanuts
2 tablespoons fresh lemon juice
1/2 teaspoon salt

1. In a medium frying pan over medium-high heat, heat the oil. Add the garlic, cayenne pepper, and chili powder to the pan. Turn heat down to medium. Cook 2 minutes, stirring constantly. Add the peanuts, lemon juice, and salt to the pan. Stir until peanuts are well coated. Serve warm.

Salads

Lesotho Mealie Meal Salad

YIELD: 6 SERVINGS

This recipe from Lesotho uses mealie meal (cornmeal), the staple crop of this South African enclave. Serve the loaf sliced and chilled on a bed of lettuce, with dollops of mayonnaise.

1^1/2 cups mealie meal (cornmeal)

4 cups boiling water

2 carrots, peeled and trimmed

2 eggs

1 onion

2 small tomatoes

1 teaspoon salt

1 teaspoon black pepper

^{1}/8 teaspoon cayenne pepper

Butter, for pan

1. Place the cornmeal in a large mixing bowl; slowly add the boiling water, 1 cup at a time, and stir together until smooth but thick, about 5 minutes. Allow the mixture to cool.

2. Place the carrots and eggs in a pot and cover with water. Bring to a boil and cook until the carrots are tender and the eggs are hard-cooked, about 10 minutes. Shell the eggs and chop them with the carrots, onion, and tomatoes until fine. Combine the egg and vegetable mixture with the cornmeal paste. Season the mixture with the salt, black pepper, and cayenne pepper.

3. Pat the mixture into a lightly buttered loaf pan. Refrigerate until ready to serve.

Salada de Quiabo (Okra Salad)

YIELD: 6 SERVINGS

When I was younger, the thought of eating okra would make me cringe. Like many people, I thought of it as a limp, slimy vegetable. When properly prepared, though, okra can have a wonderful taste and texture. This salad is popular in Brazil, where many slaves were brought.

1 package (about 10 ounces) frozen whole okra pods
1 tablespoon fresh lemon juice
1 tablespoon chopped onion
1/2 cup prepared French dressing
1/2 teaspoon black pepper

1/2 pound salad greens (shredded cabbage, endive, watercress, romaine, spinach, or lettuce)
2 hard-cooked eggs, sliced into rounds
6 whole black olives

1. Cook okra according to the package directions. Drain and cool.

2. Place okra in a medium bowl and sprinkle with the lemon juice. Add the onion, French dressing, and black pepper. Toss gently until okra is well coated. Divide salad greens among 6 small plates. Arrange okra on top of the greens. Add a few slices of egg. Place an olive in the center of each plate. Refrigerate until ready to serve.

South African Cucumber and Chile Salad

YIELD: 6 SERVINGS

Before eating, open thy mouth. —Wolof proverb

2 large cucumbers, peeled and thinly sliced
1 1/2 teaspoons salt
3 tablespoons red wine vinegar

1/2 teaspoon sugar
1 teaspoon finely chopped fresh hot green chile

1. In a bowl, combine the cucumbers, salt, 1 tablespoon of the vinegar, and 1/4 teaspoon of the sugar. Marinate the mixture 30 minutes at room temperature.

2. Using a paper towel, squeeze the excess moisture out of the cucumbers and remove them to a serving bowl. Combine the cucumbers with the remaining 2 tablespoons vinegar, the remaining 1/4 teaspoon sugar, and the chiles. Toss until the cucumbers are thoroughly coated. Serve chilled or at room temperature.

Yemiser Selatta (Ethiopian Lentil Salad)

YIELD: 4 SERVINGS

In Ethiopia, lentil salad is traditionally served during Lent, either alone or with Ethiopian injera bread (page 57).

1¼ cups (about 1/2 pound) dried lentils
1 teaspoon plus a pinch salt
3 tablespoons red wine vinegar
2 tablespoons vegetable oil
1/4 teaspoon black pepper

8 large shallots, peeled and halved
   lengthwise
1 fresh hot green chile, stemmed,
   seeded, and julienned

1. Wash the lentils in a sieve under cold running water. Bring a medium pot of water to a boil; add a pinch of salt. Add the lentils. The water should cover them by 2 or 3 inches. Partly cover the pot. Simmer 25 to 30 minutes, or until the lentils are firm but tender. Drain the lentils in a sieve, cool them under cold running water, drain them again, and set them aside.

2. In a deep bowl, combine the vinegar, oil, 1 teaspoon salt, and the black pepper. Whisk until well blended. Stir in the lentils, shallots, and chile until they are well coated. Marinate the salad at room temperature for at least 30 minutes, stirring gently from time to time. Serve at room temperature.

North African Orange Salad

YIELD: 6 SERVINGS

This refreshing salad, common to North Africa, presents beautifully and is simple to prepare.

2 cups shredded iceberg lettuce

1 large onion, thinly sliced

8 Greek olives, pitted and chopped

2 large oranges, peeled and thinly sliced

DRESSING:

2 tablespoons olive oil

2 tablespoons fresh lemon juice

1/8 teaspoon salt

1/8 teaspoon cayenne pepper

1. Toss the lettuce, onion, and olives in a salad bowl. Arrange the orange slices on top.

2. To make the dressing: Whisk together the oil, lemon juice, salt, and cayenne pepper and drizzle over the salad. If not serving immediately, refrigerate salad and dressing separately.

South African Date and Onion Salad

YIELD: 4 SERVINGS

This salad makes a delightful contrast to a spicy main dish.

3 tablespoons red wine vinegar

1/2 teaspoon salt

1/4 teaspoon sugar

1/2 pound pitted dates, quartered

1 medium onion, thinly sliced

1. In a medium serving bowl, stir together the vinegar, salt, and sugar until the sugar is completely dissolved. Add the dates and onion and stir until they are evenly coated. Refrigerate in an airtight container. This salad is best when served within 24 hours of preparation.

Stews and Soups

Efo (Nigerian Spinach Stew)

YIELD: 8 SERVINGS

I love stew, and this delightful combination of fish and spinach is a lovely way to warm up on a winter's day. It's worth a little extra time to make your own shrimp stock from the shrimp shells, as it infuses the soup with even more flavor. Just gently simmer the shells from the shrimp in some water and add some onions, bay leaves, carrots, peppercorns, lemon slices, and dried or fresh herbs. Strain the stock and proceed with the recipe.

1 pound white fish fillets (tilapia, catfish, sole, or flounder)
3 cups water or shrimp stock
1/4 teaspoon salt
1/4 cup peanut oil
1 large onion, diced

2 medium tomatoes, diced
1/4 teaspoon dried thyme
1/4 teaspoon cayenne pepper
1 1/2 pounds spinach, washed and shredded
1/2 pound medium shrimp, cleaned, shelled, and deveined

1. Cut the fish fillets into small pieces and place them in a large, uncovered pot. Add 3 cups water or shrimp stock and the salt. Simmer the fish until the water partially evaporates, about 10 minutes.

2. Add the peanut oil, onion, tomatoes, thyme, and cayenne pepper. Simmer 5 minutes, then add the spinach. Do not add any more water unless the mixture begins to stick. Cook over low heat, 10 minutes, stirring occasionally, until the spinach is tender. Add in the shrimp and cook another 2 to 3 minutes, until the shrimp has turned pink but is still tender.

Congolese Green Papaya Soup

YIELD: 4 SERVINGS

Papayas are also known as pawpaws and tree melons. Green papayas are good for soups, pickles, and chutneys. Papayas can be eaten raw after they have become fairly soft and the skin has turned from green to yellow.

2 tablespoons butter

1 small onion, minced

2 cups chicken broth

2 large green papayas, peeled, sliced
    lengthwise, seeded, and diced
    (about 2 cups)

1 teaspoon salt

1/4 teaspoon cayenne pepper

1/4 cup milk

1 teaspoon cornstarch

1. In a large saucepan, melt the butter over medium heat. Add the onion and sauté until transparent. Add the broth, papaya, salt, and cayenne pepper to the saucepan and simmer until the papaya is tender, about 8 minutes.

2. Pour the mixture into a blender or food processor. Cover the top of the blender with a towel to prevent any of the hot liquids from spilling out. Pulse the mixture a few times and then start the machine on low speed and puree until the mixture is smooth. Return the mixture to the saucepan.

3. Pour the milk into a small bowl and slowly whisk in the cornstarch, stirring until smooth. Add the cornstarch mixture to the papaya to thicken the soup. Simmer the soup over low heat, stirring constantly, 5 minutes.

Froi (Ghanian Eggplant Stew)

YIELD: 4 SERVINGS

In Africa eggplants are often called garden eggs. Eggplant and fish make a tasty combination. The tablespoon of poultry seasoning may sound strange; however, I've found that it's a wonderful flavoring for fish. After all, taste is the true test of any meal. You can make shrimp stock by gently simmering the shells from the shrimp in some water and adding some onions, bay leaves, carrots, peppercorns, lemon slices, and dried or fresh herbs.

2 pounds white fish fillets (tilapia, catfish, sole, or flounder)
1 tablespoon poultry seasoning
3 tablespoons olive oil
1 large eggplant, peeled and cut into 1/2-inch cubes
1/2 large onion, chopped
1/2 green bell pepper, seeded and diced
2 tomatoes, quartered
1/2 tablespoon salt
1 teaspoon black pepper
1/4 teaspoon crushed red pepper flakes
1/2 pound shrimp, shelled and deveined
1 cup shrimp stock or water

1. Preheat the oven to 350 degrees. Wash the fillets and pat dry. Sprinkle with the poultry seasoning; set aside.

2. In a heavy skillet over moderate heat, heat the oil until hot but not smoking; cook the eggplant, onion, bell pepper, and tomatoes until the onions are soft but not brown. Add the salt, black pepper, and the red pepper flakes. Reduce the heat to low, cover the skillet tightly, and simmer until the vegetables are tender, about 5 minutes. Put the vegetables in a blender or food processor and puree until smooth.

3. Pour the pureed vegetables into a 6-quart casserole or Dutch oven. Layer the fillets over the vegetables and arrange the shrimp over the fillets. Add the stock or water, cover tightly, and bake 20 to 25 minutes.

Groundnut Stew

YIELD: 8 SERVINGS

> In Africa peanuts are called groundnuts. This is one of the most popular stews on the continent. It is delicious when served with brown rice, rice foofoo (page 59), or Ghana kelewele (page 20).

2 tablespoons peanut or vegetable oil
1 (3¹/2- to 4-pound) fryer chicken, cleaned
 and cut up, or 8 whole bone-in
 chicken breasts
2 cloves garlic, minced
1 (6-ounce) can tomato paste
2 cups water

1 teaspoon curry powder
1 teaspoon dried thyme
¹/2 teaspoon cayenne pepper, or to taste
¹/2 cup chunky peanut butter
¹/2 pound medium shrimp, shelled and
 deveined

1. In a heavy pot or Dutch oven, heat the oil over high heat until hot but not smoking. Reduce the heat to moderate. Add the chicken, cooking a few pieces at a time so that the meat browns evenly. Remove it from the pot when browned all over. When all the chicken is browned, drain off all but 2 tablespoons of the fat in the pot. Add the garlic and stir until the garlic is golden, about 2 minutes.

2. In a separate bowl, combine the tomato paste with 2 cups water and add to the pot, along with the curry powder, thyme, and cayenne. Stir until the mixture is smooth. Let the stew simmer 5 minutes. Remove 3 tablespoons of the stew liquid and mix it with the peanut butter until smooth. Slowly add the thinned peanut butter to the stew, stirring until it is well combined. Return the chicken pieces to the stewpot. Cover and simmer the stew on low heat until the chicken is fork-tender, about 30 to 40 minutes. Add the shrimp and continue cooking the stew until the shrimp are done, about 3 to 5 minutes.

Muhogo Tamu (East African Beef and Cassava Stew)

YIELD: 6 SERVINGS

Cassava, which is also known as yucca or manioc, is the tuber from which tapioca is made. Cassava is a staple food in Africa. It is either cooked whole, pounded into a pulp, or ground into a coarse flour.

As the African captives traveled, cassava has traveled, too. It is known as mandioca in Brazil, and is also commonly used in West Indian dishes. Cassava is a tasty way to thicken soups and stews, and provides a nutritious starch when served as a side dish. Most grocery stores stock it, and you can often find it both whole and powdered in Asian markets.

1 1/2 teaspoons salt

1 pound cassava, peeled and cut into 1/2-inch cubes

1 1/2 pounds stew beef, cubed

1 teaspoon black pepper

1/4 cup peanut oil

1 small onion, minced

1 teaspoon ground turmeric

2 medium tomatoes, cut into wedges

1 cup water

1 cup coconut milk

1 tablespoon chopped jalapeno pepper

3 tablespoons chopped cilantro

1. Fill a medium pot with water and add 1/2 teaspoon salt. Bring the water to a boil and add the cassava. Boil the cassava until it is fork-tender but not mushy, about 10 minutes. Drain in a colander and set aside.

2. Season the stew meat with the remaining teaspoon salt and the black pepper. In a skillet, heat the oil over moderate heat until hot but not smoking; brown the beef, turning frequently. Drain on paper towels. Add the onion to the oil that remains in the pan and cook, stirring frequently, until golden brown. Add the turmeric and cook, stirring, 1 minute.

3. Return the beef to the skillet. Add the tomatoes and 1 cup water, and stir to combine. Increase the heat to high and bring the mixture to a boil. Reduce the heat to low and simmer, partly covered, about 1 hour, or until the beef is tender.

4. In a bowl, combine the coconut milk, chile, and cilantro and pour the mixture into the skillet. Add the cassava and combine all the ingredients well. Simmer, partly covered, 10 to 15 minutes.

Also pictured: Rice FooFoo (page 59)

Lamb Taushe

YIELD: 6 SERVINGS

Taushe is a stew served in most parts of Africa. You can substitute beef for the lamb if you desire. Ground peanuts are a common ingredient in African soups and stews. They add protein to the dish and help to thicken and add flavor to the taushe.

1/4 cup vegetable oil

2 pounds boneless stew lamb, cubed

1 large tomato, peeled and chopped

1 large onion, diced

4 scallions, chopped

1 teaspoon salt

1 tablespoon black pepper

1/2 teaspoon cayenne pepper

2 cups water

1 1/4 cups diced pumpkin (about 1 pound), or 2 sweet potatoes, peeled and diced into 2-inch cubes

1/4 cup smooth peanut butter

1/2 pound spinach, washed and shredded

1. In a large, heavy pot, heat the oil over medium-high heat until hot but not smoking. Brown the lamb pieces all over. Add the tomato, onion, scallions, salt, black pepper, cayenne pepper, and 2 cups water. Reduce heat, cover, and simmer 30 minutes.

2. Add the pumpkin or sweet potatoes and simmer another 20 minutes. Stir in the peanut butter; add the spinach and simmer an additional 20 minutes, until the vegetables are tender.

Doro We't (Chicken Stew)

YIELD: 6 SERVINGS

Doro we't is a very popular Ethiopian stew. It is usually served on special occasions and has several variations. Ethiopian injera (page 57), the pancake-like national bread, is always served with doro we't and is used to absorb every drop of the flavorful sauce.

1 (3½- to 4-pound) chicken, cleaned, skinned, and cut into 8 pieces
1 lime, quartered
1 cup (2 sticks) butter or niter kebbeh (page 15)
1 red onion, chopped
½ teaspoon cayenne pepper

2 cups water
¼ teaspoon ground cardamom
2 teaspoons garlic powder
½ teaspoon ground ginger
1 teaspoon salt
¼ teaspoon black pepper
6 medium hard-cooked eggs, sliced

1. Place the chicken pieces in a bowl and add water to cover. Gently squeeze the juice from the quartered lime over the chicken and add the lime pieces to the bowl. Set aside.

2. In a skillet, melt the butter or heat the niter kebbeh over low heat and sauté the onion until golden brown. Add the cayenne pepper and increase the heat to medium-low. Add 2 cups water, the cardamom, garlic powder, and ginger to the skillet. Stir well and add the chicken pieces. Cook about 30 minutes, stirring occasionally, until the chicken is tender. Do not overcook. Sprinkle in the salt and stir. Remove the chicken from the skillet and place in a serving bowl. Pour the sauce over the chicken and sprinkle with black pepper. Arrange the hard-cooked eggs on top.

Palava Stew

YIELD: 8 TO 10 SERVINGS

Palava stew was my first introduction to African food. It has a wonderful, spicy flavor and is usually served with a dumpling-like side dish called rice foofoo (page 59). For a delightful change, substitute smoked turkey for the chicken.

1 pound stew beef, cut into 1^1/2-inch chunks

1 pound dark meat chicken, cut at joints

1 teaspoon salt

1 teaspoon curry powder

^{1}/2 teaspoon to 2 tablespoons cayenne pepper, to taste

^{1}/2 cup peanut oil

1 large onion, thinly sliced

4 cups water

^{1}/2 cup sliced okra, fresh or frozen

1^1/2 cups packed chopped spinach

1^1/2 cups packed chopped mustard greens

1. Sprinkle the beef and chicken with the salt, curry powder, and cayenne pepper. In a Dutch oven, heat the oil over medium-high heat until hot but not smoking; add the onion and brown the beef and chicken a few pieces at a time removing the meat once it has browned. Pour off any remaining oil.

2. Return all the beef and chicken to the pot and add the remaining ingredients. Cover and bring to a boil over high heat. Reduce the heat to low and simmer, stirring occasionally, 20 minutes, or until the vegetables are tender and the meat is thoroughly cooked.

Main Dishes

Chicken Tagine with Almonds

YIELD: 4 SERVINGS

Rooster, do not be so proud. Your mother was only an eggshell. —Ashanti proverb

5 tablespoons butter
1/4 cup olive oil
1 clove garlic, crushed
1/4 teaspoon ground ginger
1/4 teaspoon ground saffron
1/2 cup water, plus additional water
   as needed

1 (2- to 3-pound) broiler/fryer chicken,
   quartered
1 teaspoon ground coriander
1/4 cup sliced almonds

1. In a skillet, melt 4 tablespoons of the butter over medium heat. Add the oil, garlic, ginger, and saffron, and cook briefly until the garlic is golden. Slowly add 1/2 cup water, then add the chicken pieces. Add more water until the chicken is partly covered. Add the coriander and cover the skillet with a tight-fitting lid. Reduce the heat to low and simmer until the chicken is tender, about 45 minutes. Remove the chicken from the skillet and arrange on a serving dish.

2. Increase the heat to high and bring the sauce to a boil until it is reduced by half, stirring frequently. Pour the sauce over the chicken.

3. In a small pan over moderate heat, melt the remaining 1 tablespoon butter. Add the almonds and cook over medium heat, stirring frequently to prevent burning, until golden brown and toasted, about 3 minutes. Sprinkle the browned almonds over the chicken.

Camarao à Lauretia (Mozambique Shrimp)

YIELD: 4 SERVINGS

I call this dish African fast food, because it's easy to prepare, delicious, and a delightful change from the typical ways shrimp is prepared in America.

12 jumbo shrimp, shelled and deveined,
   tails left intact
1/4 cup olive oil
1/2 onion, chopped
1 large clove garlic, chopped
1 teaspoon salt
1 teaspoon black pepper

1 teaspoon sweet paprika
1 teaspoon ground cumin
2/3 cup canned drained and chopped
   tomatoes
2 tablespoons ground coriander
2 cups unsweetened coconut milk

1. Wash the shrimp under cold running water and drain on paper towels. In a heavy skillet, heat the oil over medium-high heat until hot but not smoking. Sauté the onion and garlic until translucent but not brown. Add the shrimp and season it with the salt, black pepper, paprika, and cumin. Sauté 2 minutes. Remove the shrimp and vegetables from the pan and set aside.

2. Add the tomatoes and coriander to the pan. Simmer 2 to 3 minutes then stir in the coconut milk. Simmer the sauce 5 to 7 minutes. Add the shrimp and vegetables back to the pan. Simmer over low heat 3 to 4 minutes. Serve over rice.

Congolese Chicken Moambe

YIELD: 4 SERVINGS

Chicken moambe has been called the national dish of the Congo. It has many variations, but I like this version best because the seasonings blend so well. This recipe has become one of my signature dishes; I use it often as a delicious example of African cooking at its finest. You can use a store-bought rotisserie chicken and simmer it in the sauce for a modern twist on this traditional recipe.

1 (3-pound) boiler/fryer chicken, quartered
1 teaspoon salt
1/2 teaspoon cayenne pepper
1 tablespoon butter
1 onion, minced

1/4 teaspoon ground nutmeg
1/2 cup canned tomato sauce
1/2 cup smooth peanut butter
1 cup white rice

1. Season the chicken with the salt and cayenne pepper and put it in a large pot. Pour in enough water to just cover the chicken completely. Heat the water to just under a boil over medium-high heat. Reduce the heat to a very low simmer, so that 1 or 2 bubbles break the surface of the broth about once a minute. Skim any fat and scum from the surface with a ladle, large spoon, or skimmer. Cover and cook about 1 hour, or until the chicken is cooked through but not dry. Reserve the chicken stock and use it to cook the rice.

2. In a large saucepan, melt the butter over medium-high heat, and sauté the onion until golden brown. Add the nutmeg and tomato sauce and simmer about 5 minutes. Add the chicken and simmer over low heat, covered, about 15 minutes.

3. Place the peanut butter in a small bowl and microwave it until slightly liquefied, about 2 minutes. Stir the peanut butter into the tomato sauce and simmer for another 10 minutes.

4. Place 2 cups of the reserved stock and the rice in a pot and bring to boil. Cover, reduce heat to low, and cook without uncovering the pot, for 15 minutes. Let stand uncovered for 5 minutes before serving.

Dodo and Sima (Kenya Steak Supreme with Cornmeal Balls)

YIELD: 4 SERVINGS

The Kenyan steak dish called dodo is usually served smothered in tomato gravy and surrounded by sima, which are dumpling-like balls of cornmeal dough. It is truly a supreme meal. To serve, dip the dumplings in the sauce.

DODO:
2 tablespoons peanut oil
1 pound sirloin steak, cut into 4 steaks
1 1/2 cups water
1 tomato, peeled and chopped
1/4 teaspoon baking soda
1 teaspoon salt
1/2 teaspoon black pepper
1/2 cup smooth peanut butter

SIMA:
1 tablespoon butter, plus more for pan
2 cups water
1 1/2 cups cornmeal
1 egg
1/4 cup milk

1. To prepare the dodo: In a skillet, heat the oil over medium-high heat until hot but not smoking; brown the steaks on both sides. Remove the skillet from the heat. Add 1 cup of the water, the tomato, baking soda, salt, and black pepper, and return the skillet to the heat. Simmer over low heat until about 1/2 cup liquid remains, 20 to 30 minutes.

2. In a small bowl, combine the peanut butter with the remaining 1/2 cup water until smooth. Add to the meat and simmer until the steak is tender, about 30 minutes.

3. To prepare the sima: Grease a cookie sheet lightly with butter. In a saucepan, bring 2 cups water to a boil and slowly stir in the cornmeal. Reduce the heat to low and continue stirring until the cornmeal thickens. Add the butter and continue stirring, about 10 minutes, until the mixture is quite stiff. Remove from the heat. In a small bowl, beat together the egg and milk. Measure out tablespoons of the cornmeal dough and dip them in the egg mixture, placing each sima on the prepared cookie sheet. Brown the sima under a broiler, 2 to 3 minutes. Arrange the dodo on a platter and surround it with the sima.

Ghana Jollof Rice

YIELD: 8 SERVINGS

Although this version of jollof rice hails from Ghana, it is a popular dish in many regions of the African continent. In this version of the recipe, the rice is cooked along with the other ingredients, rather than as a separate starch. Jollof contains just about everything you need for a globally inspired, one-dish meal.

2 cups water or chicken broth

1 (3-pound) fryer chicken, cut into 8 pieces

2 (16-ounce) cans stewed tomatoes

2 teaspoons salt

1 teaspoon black pepper

3/4 cup cubed, cooked, smoked ham

1 cup uncooked rice

1 large onion, sliced

3 cups shredded green cabbage

1/2 pound fresh green beans, quartered and stems removed, or 1 (10- ounce) package frozen or 1 (8-ounce) can, drained

1/2 teaspoon ground cinnamon

1/4 teaspoon cayenne pepper

1. Pour 2 cups water or broth into a large pot. Add the chicken, tomatoes, salt, and black pepper. Cover, bring to a boil, then reduce the heat and simmer gently, 30 minutes. Stir in the ham, rice, onion, cabbage, green beans, cinnamon, and cayenne pepper.

2. Bring to a boil, then reduce heat to low. Cover and simmer until the chicken is fork-tender and the rice is cooked, 25 to 30 minutes.

Nigerian Roast Pepper Chicken

YIELD: 4 SERVINGS

The old woman looks after the hens and the hens look after the old woman [by laying eggs] —Ashanti proverb

1 (3-pound) fryer chicken, quartered

1/2 cup peanut oil

1/2 teaspoon cayenne pepper

1 teaspoon salt

1 (4-ounce) jar pimientos, drained and diced

1 onion, minced

1 tomato, peeled and diced

1. Preheat the oven to 400 degrees. Brush the chicken pieces all over with the peanut oil, then season with the cayenne pepper and salt. Put the chicken in a baking dish and sprinkle with the pimientos, onion, and tomato. Bake until brown and cooked through, 45 minutes to 1 hour.

Ghana Baked Fish with Tomato Sauce

YIELD: 4 SERVINGS

1/4 cup plus 1 tablespoon peanut oil

2 bay leaves

2 black peppercorns

2 cloves garlic, chopped

1 (2-pound) whole red snapper, cleaned
    and scaled

2 tablespoons fresh lemon juice

1 1/2 medium onions, chopped

2 teaspoons salt

1/2 teaspoon cayenne pepper

2 large tomatoes, peeled and chopped

2 teaspoons ketchup

1 teaspoon black pepper

1. Preheat the oven to 350 degrees. To prepare the seasoned oil: Place a small saucepan over medium-high heat; pour in 1/4 cup oil and heat for 1 minute until slightly warm. Remove the pan from the heat and add the bay leaves, peppercorns, and garlic and let the spices infuse the peanut oil, 30 minutes to 1 hour.

2. Strain the peanut oil and discard the solids. Wash and dry the fish and rub it inside and out with the seasoned oil, the lemon juice, and half the chopped onion. Sprinkle the fish with 1 teaspoon salt and the cayenne pepper. Bake until the flesh of the fish is opaque at the thickest part (test by inserting the tip of a knife into the thick part), 30 to 40 minutes.

3. To prepare the tomato sauce: Heat 1 tablespoon oil in a sauté pan over high heat until hot but not smoking; sauté the tomatoes and remaining onion until the onion is soft. Add the ketchup and black pepper. Simmer 10 minutes, stirring frequently. Spoon the sauce over the baked fish.

Moushkaki (Somali Barbecue)

YIELD: 4 SERVINGS

Somalia was just a distant place on the map to me until American troops were sent there to assist the Somalis during their country's time of war and famine. Somalis are traditionally a nomadic people, and this recipe reflects that way of life. Moushkaki is easy to prepare and is traditionally cooked over an open fire, making this the perfect recipe for a modern barbecue.

1/2 cup fresh lemon juice
1 clove garlic, crushed
1/2 teaspoon ground ginger
1/2 teaspoon black pepper

1/4 teaspoon cayenne pepper
1 teaspoon salt
2 pounds stew beef, cut into 1-inch cubes

1. In a bowl, combine all the ingredients except the beef. Add the beef, stir to coat, and refrigerate 6 to 8 hours, stirring occasionally.

2. Start the charcoal for the grill. Thread the beef onto skewers. When the charcoal has become partly white with ash, grill the beef until brown, turning frequently, about 10 minutes.

Bamia (Lamb with Okra)

YIELD: 4 SERVINGS

3 tablespoons olive oil
2 (10-ounce) packages frozen okra,
    thawed and drained
1 pound stew lamb, cut into 1-inch cubes
2 cloves garlic, chopped

2 to 3 tomatoes, peeled and chopped
1 teaspoon salt
1/2 teaspoon black pepper
1 cup water or chicken broth

1. In a saucepan, heat the oil over medium-high heat until hot but not smoking. Add the okra and sauté until brown. Add the lamb, garlic, tomatoes, salt, black pepper, and water or broth. Cover, reduce the heat, and simmer about 1 1/2 hours, until the lamb is tender.

Also pictured: South African Cucumber and Chile Salad (page 24)

Moroccan Beef Tagine with Artichokes

YIELD: 6 SERVINGS

Tagine refers to a type of stew, as well as the pot it is cooked and served in. The tagine has a removable conical cover with a hole at the top to release the steam. The bottom part of the tagine is flat in the center with curved sides to hold in the cooking liquids. Using a tagine is like cooking in a beautiful piece of earthenware artwork.

Traditionally, the tagine dish is placed on top of hot coals that are covered with ash; the stew is cooked slowly to allow enough time for the spices to mingle to perfection. This recipe uses a covered skillet in place of a traditional tagine to accommodate modern American cooks.

3 tablespoons olive oil

2 pounds stew beef, cubed

1 onion, chopped

2 tomatoes, sliced

1 teaspoon salt

1/2 teaspoon ground ginger

1/2 teaspoon black pepper

1/4 cup chopped fresh parsley

1/4 teaspoon ground cinnamon

1 1/2 cups low-sodium beef broth

12 fresh artichoke hearts, or 2 (10-ounce) packages frozen artichoke hearts or 1 (8-ounce) jar artichoke hearts

1. In a skillet, heat the oil over high heat until hot but not smoking; brown the beef. Add the onion and cook over moderate heat until the onion is golden brown. Add the tomatoes and seasonings. Reduce the heat, cover with a tight-fitting lid, and simmer 25 minutes, stirring occasionally. Add the broth and artichoke hearts. Continue to simmer the tagine over low heat until the artichokes are tender (about 30 minutes if you use fresh, 15 to 20 minutes if you use frozen or canned). Serve with couscous or rice, if desired.

Yassa au Poulet (West African Lemon-Marinated Chicken)

YIELD: 4 SERVINGS

This wonderful West African dish is simmered in a savory lemon and onion marinade. Add a pot of rice and a crisp, green salad and you'll have a memorable meal.

2 large onions, sliced

3 cloves garlic, minced

1 hot green chile, minced, or to taste

1 tablespoon salt

1/2 teaspoon ground ginger

1 teaspoon black pepper

1 cup fresh lemon juice

1 1/4 cups water or chicken broth

5 tablespoons peanut oil

1 (2- to 3-pound) fryer chicken, quartered

1. In a large baking dish, combine the onion, garlic, chile, salt, ginger, and black pepper. Stir in the lemon juice, 1 cup water or broth, and 1 tablespoon oil. Coat the chicken pieces in the marinade, and refrigerate for at least 4 hours, turning the pieces every 1/2 hour.

2. Remove the chicken from the marinade, and reserve the marinade. Pat the pieces dry with paper towels. In a skillet, heat the remaining 4 tablespoons oil over medium-high heat until hot but not smoking. Brown the chicken in the oil, a few pieces at a time, turning frequently to brown evenly. Pour off all but about 2 tablespoons oil from the skillet and remove it from the heat.

3. Using the back of a spoon, press the marinade through a fine sieve set over a bowl. Reheat the oil in the skillet over medium heat and add the solids from the sieve. Stirring constantly, cook the onion until it is transparent, about 5 minutes.

4. Return the chicken to the skillet and add 1/2 cup strained marinade and the remaining 1/4 cup water. Bring the mixture to a boil over high heat. Partly cover the pan, reduce the heat, and simmer about 25 minutes, or until the chicken is tender.

Mtuzi Wa Samki (Kenyan Baked Fish with Spicy Sauce)

YIELD: 4 SERVINGS

If plain water was satisfying enough, then the fish would not take the hook.
—Ashanti proverb

2 tablespoons vegetable oil

1 large onion, sliced

2 cloves garlic, chopped

1 teaspoon seeded and finely chopped
  jalapeño pepper

1 (16-ounce) can tomatoes, diced and the
  juice discarded

2 tablespoons white cider vinegar

1 1/4 teaspoons ground cumin

3/4 teaspoon ground coriander

1 teaspoon salt

4 (1-inch-thick) cod fillets or halibut
  steaks (2 pounds total)

1. Preheat the oven to 350 degrees. To prepare the sauce: In a skillet, heat the oil over high heat until hot but not smoking; sauté the onion, garlic, and jalapeño pepper until the onion is transparent. Stir in the tomatoes, vinegar, cumin, coriander, and salt. Simmer, uncovered, about 5 minutes, stirring occasionally.

2. Place the fish in an ungreased oblong baking pan. Spoon the sauce over the fish. Bake, uncovered, 25 to 30 minutes. Do not overcook.

South African Bobotie

YIELD: 8 SERVINGS

Bobotie is a traditional meal for the Afrikaners (South Africans of European, usually Dutch, ancestry). It is similar to American meatloaf and is usually served with rice. The heavy East Indian influence in this dish is the result of the Dutch slave trade in Malaysia. The Dutch traders brought East Indian spices back to Africa, and the slave cooks used the spices and cooking techniques they were familiar with to create a new cuisine in the country where they were enslaved.

2 slices firm white bread, crumbled

2 cups milk

1 1/2 pounds ground beef

2 medium onions, chopped

1 clove garlic, minced

2 tablespoons butter

1 1/2 teaspoons curry powder

1 teaspoon salt

1 tablespoon sugar

2 tablespoons fresh lemon juice

1/2 teaspoon grated lemon zest

2 tablespoons raisins

2 tablespoons sliced almonds

2 tablespoons apricot jam

2 eggs

1. Preheat the oven to 350 degrees. Soak the bread in 1 cup milk for 5 minutes. Squeeze out the excess liquid. In a large bowl, combine the bread with the ground beef.

2. In a medium skillet over medium-high heat, sauté the onions and garlic in 1 tablespoon butter until the onions are golden brown. Stir in 1 teaspoon curry powder, the salt, sugar, lemon juice, zest, raisins, almonds, and jam. Simmer the mixture 15 minutes over low heat.

3. Add the mixture to the beef in the bowl and blend in 1 egg. Grease a baking dish with the remaining tablespoon of butter. Put the mixture in the baking dish, smoothing until flat, and bake 30 minutes. Pour off the fat.

4. In a small bowl, combine the remaining egg, 1 cup milk, and 1/2 teaspoon curry powder. Pour the mixture over the meat. Reduce the oven temperature to 300 degrees. Cook the bobotie until it is done and the topping is set, 30 to 40 minutes. Do not overcook, as bobotie should be moist.

Vegetables

Dundu Oniyeri (West African Fried Yams)

YIELD: 6 SERVINGS

Yams are an important ingredient in African cooking. The long, white African yams have a distinctive taste, but they are not usually carried in American grocery stores. Some people in Nigeria believe that eating white yams will make a woman give birth to twins—a sign of luck! I've happily eaten many white yams without any change in the size of my household. Some Asian markets carry a variety of white African yams (cocoyams, water yams, and white yams) when they are in season; or you can do what my ancestors did when they arrived in America: substitute sweet potatoes.

1 quart plus 2 tablespoons water

2 teaspoons salt

2 pounds yams or sweet potatoes, peeled
    and cut into 1/2-inch slices

1 cup all-purpose flour

1 teaspoon black pepper

1/2 teaspoon ground cinnamon

1/2 teaspoon sweet paprika

2 eggs

2 tablespoons water

2 cups peanut or vegetable oil

1. Combine 1 quart water, 1 teaspoon salt, and the yams or sweet potatoes in a saucepan and bring to a boil. Cook until the yams are tender but firm, about 20 minutes. Drain in a colander.

2. On a plate, combine the flour, the remaining 1 teaspoon salt, the black pepper, cinnamon, and paprika. In a shallow bowl, combine the eggs and 2 tablespoons water. Dip the yams into the seasoned flour, then into the egg mixture, and into the flour again. Continue until all the pieces are coated.

3. In a heavy skillet, heat the oil over high heat until hot but not smoking. Fry the yams until golden brown. Remove from the pan with a slotted spoon and drain on food-safe paper towels; sprinkle with additional salt, if desired.

East African Stuffed Okra

YIELD: 4 SERVINGS

Okra is another African export to America that has become popular across the country.

12 okra, washed, tips removed but stems
    left intact
1/4 cup fresh lemon juice
2 cloves garlic, minced
2 teaspoons ground turmeric

2 teaspoons curry powder
1/4 teaspoon cayenne pepper
1 teaspoon salt, plus more to taste
1 cup vegetable oil

1. Cut the washed okra lengthwise, leaving the stem end intact so that the 2 halves remain connected. In a small bowl, combine the lemon juice with the garlic. Add the turmeric, curry powder, cayenne pepper, and salt. Stir until the mixture forms a thick paste. Spread the paste on the cut sides of the okra and press the sides together firmly.

2. In a skillet, heat the oil over high heat until hot but not smoking, and fry the okra until lightly browned. Drain the okra on food-safe paper towels and sprinkle with additional salt, if desired.

Mchicha Wa Nazi (East African Spinach)

YIELD: 4 SERVINGS

Coconut milk and peanuts give this spinach dish a wonderful flavor.

2 pounds spinach, washed and stems
    removed
1 teaspoon salt
2 tablespoons butter
1 cup chopped onion

1/2 teaspoon chopped hot green chile
1 cup coconut milk
1/2 cup finely crushed unsalted roasted
    peanuts

1. Put the wet spinach leaves and salt in a heavy pot and cover tightly. Steam the spinach over moderate heat until it is tender, about 10 minutes. Drain the spinach in a sieve, chop the leaves coarsely, and set aside.

2. In a heavy skillet over medium-high heat, melt the butter. Add the onion and chile and, stirring frequently, cook until they are soft but not brown. Add the coconut milk and peanuts and simmer over low heat, uncovered, stirring frequently, 2 to 3 minutes. Add the spinach and cook 4 or 5 minutes more.

West African Red Beans

YIELD: 6 TO 8 SERVINGS

This is the African forefather of the sassy red bean dish that is so popular in Louisiana.

1 cup dried pinto beans, picked over

2 quarts water

1¼ cups chopped onion

½ cup peanut or vegetable oil

1 cup canned drained and chopped
   whole tomatoes

1 tablespoon brown sugar

1 tablespoon tomato paste

1 large clove garlic, minced

1 teaspoon salt

1 teaspoon black pepper

¼ teaspoon cayenne pepper

1. Soak the beans overnight in 2 quarts water, or quick-soak them: Put the beans in a heavy pot and cover with 2 quarts water; bring to a boil, and boil for 2 to 3 minutes. Remove the pot from the heat and let the beans soak, uncovered, 1 hour.

2. In fresh water, bring the pot of soaked beans to a boil, then reduce the heat to low. Add ¼ cup onion and simmer, partly covered, about 1 hour, or until the beans are tender but not mushy. Drain the beans in a large sieve and set them aside.

3. In a large, heavy skillet, heat the oil over medium heat until hot but not smoking. Sauté the remaining 1 cup onion until soft and translucent but not brown. Add the tomatoes, brown sugar, tomato paste, garlic, salt, black pepper, and cayenne pepper. Stirring frequently, simmer the mixture until most of the liquid has evaporated. Stir in the beans and cook, uncovered, 5 to 10 minutes, stirring frequently.

Ugandan Spinach and Simsim
(Spinach and Sesame Seeds)

YIELD: 4 SERVINGS

3 to 4 tablespoons water
1/2 cup sesame seeds
1 teaspoon salt
1 teaspoon black pepper

2 pounds spinach, washed, stems
  removed, and chopped, or 1 (10-ounce)
  package frozen chopped spinach,
  thawed
1 tablespoon butter

1. Put 3 tablespoons water and the sesame seeds in a heavy saucepan. Stir in the salt, black pepper, and spinach and cover tightly. Bring to a boil, adding another tablespoon of water if necessary. Reduce the heat and simmer until the spinach is tender, 5 to 10 minutes. Drain the spinach in a sieve and return it to the saucepan. Toss with the butter.

Yataklete Kilkil (Ethiopian-Style Vegetables)
YIELD: 8 SERVINGS

Yataklete kilkil is traditionally served as a main course during Lent in Ethiopia. It also makes a tasty side dish.

4 cups water
1/4 teaspoon salt
6 small red-skin potatoes
3 carrots, sliced
6 scallions, chopped, including tops
1/2 cup fresh green beans, ends removed
  and cut into 1-inch lengths, or 1
  (9-ounce) package frozen cut green
  beans
1 tablespoon butter

2 medium onions, thinly sliced
1 green bell pepper, seeded and cut into
  strips
1/2 teaspoon chopped jalapeño pepper,
  ribs and seeds removed
1 clove garlic, chopped
1 teaspoon ground ginger
1 teaspoon salt
1 teaspoon black pepper

1. In a medium pot, bring 4 cups water and the salt to a boil. Meanwhile, peel and slice the potatoes. (Drop the potatoes into a bowl of cold water as you peel them to prevent discoloration.) Drop the potato slices into the boiling water. The water should cover the potatoes. Add the carrots, scallions, and green beans. Bring the vegetables to a rolling boil and cook, uncovered, 5 minutes. Drain the vegetables in a large colander, then rinse them with cold water to stop the cooking process and retain their bright color. Set them aside in the colander to drain completely.

2. In a heavy saucepan, heat the butter over medium-high heat until hot but not smoking. Cook the onion, bell pepper, and jalapeño pepper over low heat until the vegetables are soft but not brown, about 5 minutes. Add the garlic, ginger, salt, and black pepper and stir, then add the potatoes, carrots, scallions, and beans. Stir until the vegetables are coated with the butter mixture. Partly cover the pan and continue cooking about 10 minutes, or until the vegetables are crisp-tender.

Yebaqela Kik We't (Ethiopian Fava Beans)

YIELD: 6 SERVINGS

Fava beans are large legumes also known as horse beans and broad beans. Fava beans date to ancient times. They were often the main food given to the African captives during the Middle Passage—the journey from Africa to America.

2 cups fresh fava beans, washed
1/2 cup vegetable oil
2 cups chopped red onion
1 tablespoon minced garlic

1 teaspoon cayenne pepper
1/4 teaspoon ground cumin
1 teaspoon salt

1. Put the beans in a large pot and cover with water. Boil until the beans are tender but not mushy (5 to 15 minutes, depending on the freshness of the beans). Drain the beans.

2. In a skillet, heat the oil until hot but not smoking; sauté the onion and garlic. Add the cayenne, cumin, and salt. Cook until the onion has softened, about 5 minutes, stirring occasionally. Add the beans to the onion and garlic mixture and bring to a boil. Reduce the heat and simmer 5 minutes.

Breads, Dumplings, and Desserts

Moi-moi (Steamed Bean Cakes)

YIELD: 8 SERVINGS

Black-eyed peas are one of the foods that Africans contributed to American culture. Serving black-eyed peas is a wonderful way to combine our culinary history with our cultural one during Kwanzaa. Moi-moi is a West African dish. Traditionally, ground black-eyed peas were soaked overnight to remove the "eyes" on the skin of the peas. The peas were then pounded into a paste and wrapped in banana leaves before cooking. Since removing the skin robs the peas of important nutrients, this modern version is prepared with skins intact (and using small squares of aluminum foil in place of the banana leaves).

2 cups dried black-eyed peas

1 onion, coarsely chopped

1 egg

1/4 cup water

2 teaspoons chili powder

1 teaspoon salt

1. Place the black-eyed peas in a medium bowl and cover them with water. Soak the peas overnight. Drain off the water.

2. Place the peas and the remaining ingredients into the bowl of a food processor or blender. Grind until ingredients form a smooth paste. Place 2 heaping tablespoons of the pea mixture on a 4-inch square of aluminum foil. Tightly fold the ends of the foil around the mixture. Repeat with the remaining mixture. Place the foil packets into a medium pot and cover them with water. Simmer, covered, for 1 hour, until the moi-moi is firm. Carefully open the packets and serve hot or warm with spicy salsa.

Ethiopian Injera Bread

YIELD: 6 SERVINGS

Injera is a must for most Ethiopian meals. This pancake-like bread is used as a plate—the evening's meal is often literally served on the injera—and pieces of the bread are used as a spoon to eat with. The proper way to eat most Ethiopian dishes is to scoop up the meat or vegetables with a piece of injera, using only the right hand, and pop the entire injera-wrapped portion into your mouth.

Injera is traditionally made from teff, a highly nutritious cereal grain, similar to rye, which the Ethiopians also call lovegrass. Teff is ground into a flour and mixed with water to make a fermented batter-like dough. This is an easier version of the authentic recipe. It takes some practice to get it perfect, so don't get discouraged!

5 tablespoons all-purpose flour
3 cups Aunt Jemima's Deluxe Easy-Pour
   Pancake Mix

1/4 teaspoon baking soda
3 1/2 cups club soda, at room temperature
1 1/2 cups water, at room temperature

1. In a deep mixing bowl, combine the flour, pancake mix, and baking soda. Stirring constantly with a whisk or spoon, slowly pour in the club soda and water. Continue stirring until the mixture is smooth. Strain the batter by pressing it through a fine sieve set over a bowl. The batter will be thin.

2. Cook the injera as you would cook a pancake: Use a griddle, a 10-inch skillet, or an omelet pan. Warm the ungreased griddle or pan over moderate heat until it is just hot enough to set the batter without browning it. To test the heat, pour 1 tablespoon of the batter into the center of the pan. The bottom surface should solidify immediately without becoming brown. Remove the pan from the heat. Pour in about 1/4 cup batter. Tilt the pan so that the batter coats the bottom evenly. Partly cover the pan and cook the bread over moderate heat until the top is spongy, moist, and dotted with tiny air holes, about 1 minute. Check the bottom of the injera periodically. Do not let it brown or let the edges become too crisp. The bottom should be smooth, dry, and somewhat shiny.

3. When the injera is done, remove the pan from the heat. Place the injera on a platter or in a large, flat basket. Repeat the process until all the batter has been cooked. Allow one injera to drape over the edge of the platter or basket. Fold the rest of the injera into quarters and arrange them in a fan in the center. Serve immediately.

East African Sweet Potato Pudding

YIELD: 8 SERVINGS

I believe this wonderful pudding traveled to America and gradually became the basis for our traditional sweet potato pie.

1 quart water
6 medium sweet potatoes (2 pounds),
    peeled and cut into 1/2-inch cubes
3 cups milk

1 cup heavy cream
1/2 cup sugar
1/2 teaspoon ground saffron
1/2 teaspoon ground cardamom

1. In a heavy saucepan, boil 1 quart water. Drop in the sweet potatoes. Cook the potatoes, uncovered, until tender, 25 to 30 minutes. Drain the potatoes in a sieve or colander and return them to the pan. Add the milk, cream, sugar, saffron, and cardamom. Stirring frequently with a wooden spoon, bring the mixture to a boil over moderate heat.

2. Reduce the heat to low and simmer, uncovered, about 1 hour, stirring often. The pudding is done when it is smooth and is thick enough to hold its shape almost solidly in the spoon.

3. With the back of the spoon, rub the pudding through a fine sieve into a serving bowl. Refrigerate the pudding until cool. Before serving, sprinkle the top with a little additional ground cardamom.

Tanzanian Baked Bananas

YIELD: 8 SERVINGS

Sweets and desserts are not a large part of the African diet. For many years, sugar was extremely expensive in Africa, and sugary dishes were reserved for a treat during the Christmas holidays. This recipe from Tanzania makes an easy-to-prepare, healthful, and delicious dessert.

4 large, ripe, unpeeled bananas
4 tablespoons (1/2 stick) butter, melted

1/2 cup packed brown sugar
1 tablespoon fresh lemon juice

1. Preheat the oven to 425 degrees. Cut off the ends of the bananas. Place the unpeeled bananas on an ungreased cookie sheet or in a baking pan. Bake for 15 minutes, or until the skins burst and turn black. Peel the bananas and discard the skins; cut the bananas lengthwise. Mix the butter, brown sugar, and lemon juice and drizzle the mixture over the bananas.

Rice Foofoo

YIELD: 4 SERVINGS

Foofoo (also known as fufu, foufou, pap, and putu) is the starchy accompaniment to many main dishes in Africa. For generations, African women have pounded dried yams, cassava slices, corn kernels, plantain, or rice into flour to make foofoo. Foofoo has the consistency of a dumpling and is shaped into a ball. Small pieces of foofoo are pinched off, dipped into a soup or stew, and popped into the mouth. The way some Africans use foofoo to scoop up their food is practically an art. This is a simpler version of the flour-based foofoo recipes, but it is comparable in taste and texture.

2^1/$_2$ cups water, plus more as needed
1 teaspoon salt
1 cup rice

1. In a medium pot, boil the water. Add the salt and rice. Cook the rice over moderate heat until it is mushy, adding more water as needed, 10 to 15 minutes. Drain in a colander and return the rice to the pot. With a wooden spoon, mash the rice against the sides of the pot until it is smooth and stiff. Scrape into a bowl. Wet your hands and shape the rice into 4 balls.

VARIATIONS:
To make yam foofoo, boil 2 cups water and add 2 teaspoons salt. Peel and dice 3 to 4 medium yams and boil them in the water until tender. Drain in a colander. Mash the yams with a potato masher or fork until smooth. Shape into balls.

Drinks

African Fruit Punch

YIELD: 8 TO 10 SERVINGS

2¹/2 cups lemonade

1 cup orange juice

1 cup pineapple juice

1 cup papaya juice

1 cup guava juice

1. Mix all the juices together in a pitcher and chill. Serve over ice.

Chinandzi (Pineapple Drink)

YIELD: 8 TO 10 SERVINGS

1 large ripe pineapple

1 teaspoon ground ginger

1 teaspoon ground cloves

2 tablespoons sugar

5 cups boiling water

1. Peel and slice the pineapple and place it in a large heatproof bowl. Add the spices and sugar. Pour the boiling water over the ingredients. Cover the bowl and refrigerate overnight. Strain the drink into a pitcher. Serve over ice.

Moroccan Almond Milk

YIELD: 4 SERVINGS

This soothing drink is wonderful whether you serve it after dinner, along with or instead of coffee, or before bedtime.

1½ cups finely ground roasted almonds
½ cup packed brown sugar
1 cup water

2 cups milk
1 tablespoon orange zest

1. In a bowl, combine the almonds and sugar. Stir in ½ cup water and set the mixture aside for 30 minutes.

2. Pour the mixture into a blender and blend on low speed. With the blender running, slowly add the remaining ½ cup water and blend until smooth. Set the mixture aside for another 30 minutes.

3. In a saucepan, warm the milk; do not boil it. Add the orange zest. Stir the almond mixture into the milk and mix well. Serve warm.

The Pepperpot Is Never Empty

The Caribbean

From many people, one people.

—WEST INDIAN PROVERB

My Caribbean Kitchen

Like many Americans, my first visit to the Caribbean was part of a cruise I took with my husband and some friends. I loved the beauty of the Islands and the wonderful food. While my husband and friends swam, went snorkeling, and bought souvenirs, I talked with local cooks, purchased specialty spices and sauces, and expanded the Caribbean section of my abundant cookbook collection. My idea of a perfect vacation is discovering new historical sites, culinary facts, delicious recipes, and out-of-the-way restaurants while enjoying the scenery, the ocean, and the beaches.

In 2007 my husband, Michael, and I were invited to the U.S. Virgin Islands to visit St. Croix, St. Thomas, and St. John as guests of local public television station WTJX. St. Croix, St. John, and St. Thomas became U.S. territories when they were purchased for military reasons by the United States from the Danish government. These Islands are U.S. territories, so it makes traveling there almost as easy as a visit to another state. Because of the unique historical ties between the Virgin Islands and the United States, you really haven't seen America until you've seen the American Caribbean.

St. Croix quickly became my favorite of the three beautiful islands because of the lushness of the scenery, the graciousness of the Crucians who reside on the island, and the quiet comfort of the Buccaneer Resort where we spent the week. Moreover, St. Croix has an eco-conscious community and government, and a family-oriented atmosphere that we thoroughly enjoyed. St. Thomas is the perfect place for those who like a day of high-end shopping, and St. John is a nature-lover's dream.

We filmed episodes of The Kitchen Diva! with the fabulous island scenery in the background. We spent a week visiting historic sites, beaches, eco-camps; sampling the local cuisine; and talking with chefs, fishermen, farmers, and restaurant owners on the three islands. I learned a number of new recipes and cooked with unique local ingredients that I had only read about in cookbooks.

I've included a few of my favorite Caribbean recipes here in this book, including my versions of a callaloo soup prepared by a delightful fisherman and weekend chef named Paunchie, and a spicy coconutty rice that I tasted at a Rastafarian restaurant owned by the United Caribbean Association.

I've also tried to replicate the Petite Pump Room restaurant's blackened mahi mahi with sautéed onions, the Magic Kitchen's potato stuffing, the Blue Moon Café's sunset jazz spicy spareribs, and several other intriguing recipes that are examples of the abundance of good food to be found in the U.S. Virgin Islands. If you haven't had an opportunity to visit these beautiful gems of the Caribbean, I hope these delicious dishes will entice you to make a visit soon.

Caribbean Culinary History

Caribbean culture is like a pepper pot, a fantastic tradition that is an Island treasure. A pepper pot is not only a cooking vessel, but also a spicy stew made of whatever meats or vegetables the cook has at hand. Peppers and the juice of the cassava root are added to the pot. Small serving portions are removed from the pot and new ingredients added, so the pepper pot is never empty and never quite full. Years of simmering and blending give the ingredients of the pepper pot an unmatched flavor. Some pepper pots are considered so valuable that they are willed from one generation to the next.

The Islands, originally populated by the Arawak and the Carib Indians and colonized in the sixteenth and seventeenth centuries, became colonies of a number of European countries, including France, Spain, and Britain. The European demand for Caribbean products such as sugar, molasses, tea, coffee, and cocoa were the catalyst for the triangular slave trade between West Africa, Europe, and the colonies in the Americas, with about five percent ending up in North America, and Brazil becoming one of the largest recipients. The U.S. Virgin Islands were principally a Danish-owned territory with large plantations. The impact of the Danish occupation on St. Croix, St. Thomas, and St. John is evident in everything from the architecture to the food.

More than twelve million African slaves were brought to the New World between 1501 and 1870. By the second half of the seventeenth century, the slaves outnumbered their masters. The complexion of the islands, as well as the cuisine, began to change.

The slaves labored in the Caribbean sugarcane fields and in their masters' kitchens. They were chosen for their occupations based on their strength and temperament. The Spanish colonists picked their slaves from the Yoruba of Nigeria, in West Africa. The English preferred the Ashanti from the Gold Coast. The French purchased Dahomeans, Congolese, and Ibos to do their fieldwork, and the mild-mannered Mandingoes for house servants. The races intermingled, resulting in a new population of fair-skinned people called Creoles. The Creole language and cuisine are now as much a part of the Islands as palm trees and beaches. The U.S. Virgin Islands also have a large Puerto Rican population, and that cultural influence makes for an interesting and vibrant atmosphere.

The tastes and techniques of the French, Spanish, Danish, and English colonists influenced many of the recipes you will find in this section. You will also find here the curries and spices that were introduced by indentured servants brought from India.

The African influence on Caribbean cooking is evident in the preparation of jerk barbecue and the use of peppers. African slave cooks also created new recipes by combining the fruits and vegetables they transplanted from Africa with foods that were common to the Caribbean. The melding of ancient African spices and cooking techniques with European fare produced a range of Caribbean dishes whose flavors are virtually unmatched in other parts of the world.

A Marinade and a Sauce

Caribbean Marinade

YIELD: 3/4 CUP

Caribbean cooks use this basic seasoning combination along with their own favorite herbs and spices. That's why no dish tastes exactly the same from place to place. This marinade was used as early as the sixteenth century to preserve and tenderize tough cuts of meat. It adds a wonderful flavor to roasted, stewed, or braised meats. It is very similar to the combination of herbs and spices used by African cooks and is probably a variation of a slave recipe. This is enough marinade for about three pounds of meat. It's delicious mixed with hamburger meat, added to stews, or used as a marinade for pork, chicken, or fish.

1 medium onion, grated
1 clove garlic, minced
3 scallions, chopped
1/2 cup chopped celery leaves
1/4 cup apple cider vinegar or malt vinegar

1/4 cup water
1 tablespoon brown sugar
1 tablespoon soy sauce
1 teaspoon cayenne pepper

1. Combine all the ingredients together and store in an airtight, nonmetallic container. This marinade can be rubbed into any type of meat. Let the meat stand in the marinade at room temperature for 1 hour, turning frequently, before baking, braising, or barbecuing.

2. To make a sauce or gravy for baked or braised meats, scrape the remaining marinade from the surface of the cooked meat. Combine the cooked marinade with any juices that have collected in the bottom of the baking pan. These ingredients can be used as a sauce, or thicken them with a little flour and water as needed to make gravy.

Salsa Roja Para Frijoles Negros
(Sweet Pepper Sauce for Black Beans)

YIELD: ABOUT 4 CUPS

This salsa is a great way to spice up a bowl of black beans.

1 cup olive oil

1 1/2 cups peeled and chopped tomatoes

2 cloves garlic, minced

1 teaspoon salt

1 teaspoon black pepper

1/2 teaspoon cayenne pepper

1/2 teaspoon dried oregano

1/2 teaspoon sugar

1/2 cup tomato puree
   liquid reserved

1/4 cup white vinegar

1. In a saucepan, heat the oil over medium-high heat until hot but not smoking; add the tomatoes. Stir with a wooden or rubber spoon about 5 minutes, or until they are cooked to a soft pulp. Add the remaining ingredients except the vinegar and simmer over low heat, stirring occasionally. When the sauce has thickened, remove the pan from the heat and stir in the vinegar.

Salads and Snacks

Shrimp Salad with Coconut Cream

YIELD: 8 SERVINGS

No Caribbean dinner would be complete without a dish containing coconut or shellfish. This salad combines both, with appetizing results.

1 cup milk
1 cup grated unsweetened coconut,
　fresh or packaged
1 tablespoon vegetable oil
2 green bell peppers, seeded and chopped
2 shallots, minced

1 tablespoon chopped peanuts
2 tablespoons soy sauce
1 teaspoon salt
2 pounds medium shrimp, cooked
　and shelled

1. In a saucepan, combine the milk and coconut and bring the mixture to a boil. Remove from the heat immediately and set aside for 30 minutes. Press the mixture through a sieve to extract the cream. Discard the pulp.

2. In a skillet, heat the oil over high heat until hot but not smoking, and sauté the peppers and shallots until soft, about 3 to 5 minutes. Remove from the heat and add the peanuts, soy sauce, and salt. Stir in the cream from the coconut. Arrange the shrimp on a platter and pour the dressing over them. Chill and serve.

Green Papaya Salad

YIELD: 4 SERVINGS

Papaya, or pawpaw, is a South American import to the Islands. Although green papayas are fairly bland, when mixed with other fruits, vegetables, or spices they enhance the flavor of a dish. Green papaya tastes a little like summer squash and is often used as a vegetable of sorts, as it is in this salad.

2 large green papayas, peeled, seeded,
and diced (about 2 cups)
1¼ teaspoons salt
½ teaspoon dry mustard
1 teaspoon chopped parsley
1 teaspoon fresh lime juice

1 teaspoon black pepper
3 hard-cooked eggs, chopped
2 whole red pimientos, drained and
chopped
1½ tablespoons mayonnaise
4 crisp lettuce leaves

1. Place the papaya and ¼ teaspoon salt in a small saucepan. Cover with water and simmer until the papaya is tender, about 20 minutes. Drain and refrigerate until chilled, about 15 minutes.

2. In a bowl, combine the mustard, parsley, lime juice, the remaining teaspoon salt, the pepper, eggs, pimiento, and mayonnaise, then add the papaya and mix well. Serve the salad on a bed of lettuce leaves.

Fruited Cabbage

YIELD: 6 SERVINGS

Fruit and cabbage are an unusual combination, but a tasty one when prepared this way.

1½ pounds cabbage, shredded
¼ cup raisins
1 cup diced pineapple
2 medium onions, diced

1 cup water
Juice of 1 lime
1 teaspoon salt

1. In a medium saucepan, combine the cabbage with the fruit and onions. Add the water, lime juice, and salt, and bring to a boil. Simmer about 40 minutes, or until the liquid has evaporated and the cabbage is tender. Serve immediately.

Rice Salad

YIELD: 4 TO 6 SERVINGS

This salad was created from a recipe used by slave cooks from Malaysia. It's so colorful that it looks like it's all dressed up for a Jamaican jamboree. It is a perfect side dish for spicy jerk dishes and tastes best when it has had at least eight hours to marinate.

1 cup plain low-fat yogurt
1/2 cup raisins
1/4 cup minced onion
2 teaspoons curry powder
2 teaspoons salt
1 teaspoon black pepper

1 teaspoon ground turmeric
1/2 teaspoon sugar
3 cups cooked and cooled white rice
1/2 cup coarsely chopped green bell pepper
1/2 cup coarsely chopped red bell pepper
Lettuce leaves

1. In a medium bowl, combine the yogurt, raisins, onion, curry powder, salt, black pepper, turmeric, and sugar. Stir in the cold rice and bell peppers. Refrigerate to chill. Serve on a bed of lettuce leaves.

Meat Patties Wrapped in Pastry

YIELD: 12 PATTIES

Annatto (achiote) seeds are rust-red dried seeds that give cooking oil a bright orange-yellow color and a delicate flavor. They are popular in Caribbean cooking and can be found in some grocery stores and most Latino markets. The seeds must be removed from the hot oil as soon as it takes on the orange-yellow tint. You can also find pre-pared annatto or achiote oil in some markets, which you can use instead of making your own.

FILLING:

2 tablespoons vegetable oil

1 teaspoon annatto seeds, or 1 teaspoon ground saffron or turmeric

1 pound lean ground beef

1 onion, finely chopped

1 clove garlic, minced

1 cup peeled, seeded, and chopped tomato

1 teaspoon salt

1 teaspoon black pepper

1/4 teaspoon cayenne pepper

1/2 teaspoon dried thyme

2 eggs, lightly beaten

PASTRY:

21/2 cups all-purpose flour, plus more for dusting

1/8 teaspoon salt

12 tablespoons (11/2 sticks) cold unsalted butter

1/2 cup ice water

1 egg white, beaten until foamy

1. To prepare the filling: In a large frying pan, heat the oil over moderate heat until hot but not smoking; add the annatto seeds, saffron, or turmeric. Cook until the oil is orange-yellow, about 2 minutes. If using annatto seeds, remove them with a slotted spoon and discard.

2. Add the beef, breaking it up with a fork as it cooks, until it begins to brown. Add the onion and garlic and cook until the onion is soft. Add the tomato, salt, black pepper, cayenne pepper, and thyme. Cook, stirring, 5 minutes or longer, until the mixture is quite dry. Remove from the heat and stir in the eggs. Return to the heat and cook, stirring, 2 or 3 minutes. Cool to room temperature.

3. To prepare the pastry: Mix the flour and salt with a pastry blender or fork, or in the bowl of a food processor. Add the butter 1 tablespoon at a time, cutting it into the flour thoroughly. When all the butter has been added, the flour mixture should be grainy like cornmeal. Slowly

add the ice water to the flour, about 3 tablespoons at a time, using your hands or the processor to mix it after each addition until the dough forms a ball. Divide the dough in half and pat each half into a disk about 1/2 inch thick. Wrap the disks in plastic wrap and refrigerate for at least 30 minutes.

4. To assemble the patties: Preheat the oven to 425 degrees. Dust a work surface and rolling pin with flour and roll out half the dough until it is a strip about 8 inches wide and 1/8 inch thick. Using a floured coffee cup or biscuit cutter, cut the pastry into 6 circles. Place 1/2 cup of the meat mixture on one side of each circle and fold it over into a crescent. Seal the edges by pinching with your fingers or crimping with a fork. Brush with the beaten egg white and prick the tops to let steam escape. Repeat with the remaining dough. Bake on an ungreased cookie sheet 20 to 30 minutes, or until lightly browned.

Mango Vinaigrette

YIELD: ABOUT 2 CUPS

This mango-flavored vinaigrette can also be made with papaya, guava, or any other fresh tropical fruit. I've used it to dress everything from vegetables to fruit or green salads.

1 ripe mango
Juice of 1 lime
1/2 cup olive oil or vegetable oil
1/4 cup white balsamic vinegar
1 scallion, chopped

1/2 green bell pepper, chopped
1 (1-inch-long) piece of ginger, peeled
 and finely chopped
1 teaspoon salt
1/2 teaspoon black pepper

1. Peel and slice the mango and place the pieces in a food processor or blender. Add the lime juice and oil; blend to combine. Add the vinegar, scallion, green pepper, ginger, salt, and black pepper; blend to combine. Chill before serving.

Codfish Cakes (Stamp and Go)

YIELD: 12 CAKES

Stamp and go, or codfish cakes, are popular snacks and appetizers in Jamaica. The dish is so named because you can buy it from one of the many food vendors that populate Jamaican bus stops and then jump on the next bus.

1/2 pound salt codfish
1 cup all-purpose flour
1 teaspoon baking powder
1/2 teaspoon salt
1 egg, lightly beaten
3/4 cup milk

1 tablespoon butter, melted
1 tablespoon sweet paprika
1 onion, minced
1/2 teaspoon cayenne pepper
Vegetable oil for deep-frying

1. Put the codfish in a bowl and fill the bowl with warm water. Soak the fish for 2 to 3 hours to remove the salt.

2. Drain the fish and rinse in cool water; place it in a saucepan, cover with water, and bring to a boil. Simmer until the fish is tender, about 15 minutes. Drain, remove the bones and skin, and shred the fish.

3. Sift together the flour, baking powder, and salt. In a small bowl, combine the egg, milk, butter, and paprika, and stir into the dry ingredients. Add the fish, onion, and cayenne pepper and mix well.

4. Place 3 cups oil in a deep skillet or deep-fryer and heat over medium-high heat until hot but not smoking. Drop tablespoonfuls of the fish mixture into the hot oil and fry until golden brown. Drain on paper towels and serve hot.

Limbo Cakes

YIELD: 6 SERVINGS

It's much easier to make these crisp snacks than it is to do the acrobatic dance for which they are named.

4 cups water
1 tablespoon plus 1 teaspoon salt
3 or 4 large green plantains, peeled and
    sliced into 2-inch rounds
2 cups vegetable oil

1. Put 4 cups water in a large pot and add the salt. Soak the plantain slices in the salted water about 30 minutes to remove some of the starch. Drain the slices and pat dry with paper towels.

2. In a deep, heavy saucepan, heat the oil over medium-high heat until hot but not smoking; add the plantains, and cook about 5 minutes. Do not brown. Turn the plantains once. Drain on paper towels.

3. One by one, place the plantain slices on a sheet of waxed paper, cover with another sheet, and use a rolling pin or the flat side of a mallet to flatten to 1/2-inch thickness. Return the plantains to the hot oil and fry until crisp and brown. Drain on paper towels and sprinkle with salt.

Soups

Callaloo Soup

YIELD: 8 SERVINGS

During our visit to St. Croix, we kept hearing about Paunchie, a retired policeman who is now a full-time fisherman. Every weekend, Paunchie serves a Crucian menu fit for a king to the late-night party people on the island. Within hours, every bite of food disappears, so you have to get there when he starts serving at 2:00 a.m. Paunchie was kind enough to share his last serving of callaloo soup with me—but not the recipe. This is my homage to his tasty creation. Paunchie has a callaloo bush growing in his backyard, but I've substituted spinach, just in case your kitchen isn't located in the Caribbean!

2 pounds callaloo or spinach, or
   2 (10-ounce) packages frozen spinach
2 tablespoons butter
6 slices bacon, diced
1 onion, chopped
2 cloves garlic, chopped
2 stalks celery, diced
1/2 jalapeño or habanero pepper, diced
1 teaspoon salt
1 teaspoon black pepper

1/2 teaspoon dried thyme
1/4 teaspoon ground cloves
1/4 teaspoon ground nutmeg
1 cup sliced okra, fresh or frozen
4 cups chicken broth
1 pound lump crabmeat, shell pieces
   removed, or peeled, deveined shrimp
1/2 cup chopped parsley
2 tablespoons fresh lemon juice

1. Remove the stalks from the callaloo or the spinach and clean the greens by carefully immersing them in a sink filled with cold water, soaking them for a few minutes, lifting out the greens, cleaning the sink to remove the dirt and sand, and repeating the process 5 more times. You can also use already cleaned prepackaged or frozen spinach.

2. Melt the butter in a large stewpot. Add the bacon pieces and sauté, stirring frequently, until the bacon is crisp, 5 to 7 minutes. Using a slotted spoon, remove the bacon pieces to a paper towel–covered plate to drain, and set aside, reserving the butter in the pan. Add the onion, garlic, celery, jalapeño, salt, pepper, thyme, cloves, and nutmeg and sauté until the vegetables begin to soften, 3 to 5 minutes.

3. Add the okra, the callaloo or spinach, and the chicken broth. Bring the soup to a boil and cover. Reduce heat and simmer 35 to 40 minutes, until the okra is tender. Add the crabmeat or the shrimp, and the chopped parsley. Cover and simmer 5 to 7 minutes. Gently stir in the lemon juice. Pour the soup into large individual soup bowls. Place a slice of the coo coo (known as fungi in the Virgin Islands; recipe page 97) in the center of the soup, if desired. Serve immediately.

Breadfruit Soup

YIELD: 8 SERVINGS

Captain Bligh of the Bounty introduced breadfruit trees to the tropics in 1792. Despite its name, breadfruit is a vegetable, with a starchy potato-like taste and a brown seed that looks like a chestnut. While in St. Croix we visited the St. George Village Botanical Garden on an old 19th-century Danish sugarcane plantation. We spent a wonderful morning admiring all of the fantastic varieties of flora and fauna that grow there, including breadfruit trees. Ripe breadfruit are only edible when cooked. If fresh bread-fruit is not available, you can use the canned variety, or white yams or potatoes. This soup tastes good hot or cold.

1 breadfruit, peeled and cut into small
    pieces, or 1 (14- to 16-ounce) can,
    drained (available in Asian markets)
3 cups chicken broth
3 cloves garlic, minced

1 teaspoon salt
1 teaspoon black pepper
1 medium onion, chopped
1 1/2 cups heavy cream

1. Place the breadfruit, chicken broth, garlic, salt, pepper, and onion in a large pot over high heat. Bring the ingredients to a boil, reduce the heat to moderate, and stir until the soup is slightly thickened. With the back of a spoon or a potato masher, mash the breadfruit. Strain the soup, mashing any lumps through a sieve. Return the soup to the pot and add the cream. Simmer over low heat, stirring frequently, for 10 minutes.

Seafood

Crawfish Angelique

YIELD: 4 SERVINGS

You better not shake hands with a crawfish. —Slave proverb

4 slices bacon, diced
1 large onion, diced
2 stalks celery, diced
1 large green bell pepper, seeded and
    diced
1 clove garlic, minced
1 (14-ounce) can whole tomatoes with
    liquid
1 (12-ounce) can tomato juice

1 teaspoon Worcestershire sauce
2 cups water
2 bay leaves
1 teaspoon salt
$1/4$ teaspoon black pepper
$1/4$ teaspoon cayenne pepper
12 crawfish tails, cooked, meat removed
    and cubed

1. In a large pot, cook the bacon over medium heat until browned and crisp. Using a slotted spoon, remove the bacon and drain on paper towels.

2. Sauté the onion, celery, bell pepper, and garlic in the bacon fat until the vegetables are soft. Add the tomatoes and cook for 5 minutes. Add the tomato juice, Worcestershire sauce, 2 cups water, the bay leaves, salt, and the black and cayenne peppers. Simmer 10 to 15 minutes.

3. Add the crawfish and bacon and cook 3 to 4 minutes longer. Remove the bay leaves. Serve over rice.

Blackened Mahi Mahi with Sautéed Onions

YIELD: 4 SERVINGS

The Petite Pump Room is owned by Michael and Judith Watson and located on St. Thomas in the U.S. Virgin Islands. The food is wonderful and the atmosphere lovely. Their recipe for blackened mahi mahi with sautéed onions, like all the recipes at this family-owned restaurant, is a closely guarded secret. I've tried to replicate the spicy seasonings, but I urge you to visit the restaurant to try their spectacular version of this dish. The onions become sweeter as they caramelize and add a nice counterbalance to the spiciness of the fish. When you start preparing the fish, turn on the oven exhaust vent, Honey! There will be a lot of smoke while the fish is cooking, but the results are well worth it.

BLACKENED MAHI MAHI:
1/4 cup paprika
2 teaspoons dried thyme
2 teaspoons dried oregano
1 teaspoon garlic powder
1 teaspoon cayenne pepper
1 teaspoon black pepper
1 teaspoon cumin
2 teaspoons salt

4 mahi mahi fillets, thawed
   (1/2 pound each)
3 tablespoons vegetable oil

SAUTÉED ONIONS:
3 tablespoons vegetable oil
1 large onion, sliced
1 teaspoon salt
1 teaspoon black pepper
1/2 teaspoon sugar

1. To prepare the mahi-mahi: In a shallow dish, mix together the paprika, thyme, oregano, garlic powder, cayenne pepper, black pepper, cumin, and salt. Coat both sides of the fish fillets in the spice mixture and set aside to marinate, 30 minutes.

2. To prepare the onions: Using a large cast iron skillet or a griddle, heat 3 tablespoons oil over high heat until hot but not smoking. Place the onions in the pan and turn the heat to low. Sprinkle the onions with salt, pepper, and sugar. Sauté 30 minutes, stirring frequently, until the onions are golden brown and tender. Remove the onions to a plate and set aside.

3. Add 3 tablespoons oil to the pan. Heat the oil over medium-high heat until it is smoking slightly. Place the fish in the skillet or griddle and cook 5 minutes. Flip the fish and cook 3 to 4 minutes. Serve topped with the sautéed onions.

Caribbean Stuffed Red Snapper

YIELD: 6 TO 8 SERVINGS

I loved visiting the open air markets on St. Croix. Local fishermen display their fresh, colorful catches of the day a few feet away from the abundant wares at the farmer's market. When you purchase the whole red snapper for this recipe, ask to have it scaled, keeping the tail, fins, and head intact but with the backbone removed. The fish is filled from fin to fin with a flavorful herb stuffing and then coated with bread crumbs. It's fabulous!

1 (3- to 4-pound) whole red snapper
1 lime, quartered
Salt, for rubbing the fish

STUFFING:
2 cups bread crumbs
8 tablespoons (1 stick) butter, melted
1/4 cup chopped chives
1/4 cup chopped parsley
1/4 to 1/2 teaspoon cayenne pepper

1 small onion, grated
Grated zest and juice of 1 small lime
1 teaspoon salt
1 teaspoon white pepper
1 teaspoon dried thyme
1 teaspoon dried sweet marjoram

COATING:
2 egg whites
1 cup bread crumbs

1. Wash the fish and rub inside and out with the quartered lime and salt. Refrigerate at least 10 minutes. Wipe off the lime juice and salt.

2. Preheat the oven to 300 degrees. Place the fish on a sheet pan. Prepare the stuffing: Combine all the stuffing ingredients and fill the cavity of the snapper.

3. Prepare the coating: With a whisk, beat the egg whites until fluffy. Coat the fish by rubbing the egg white on it and sprinkling on the bread crumbs.

4. Bake the fish until the flesh is opaque, allowing about 10 minutes per pound. Do not overcook.

Fish Poached in Court Bouillon

YIELD: 6 SERVINGS

This is a relaxed Caribbean court bouillon, not the fancy French version. Poach the fish ten minutes per 1 inch of thickness. Do not test by flaking, since by then the fish will already be too dry.

2 cups cold water

7 tablespoons fresh lime juice

1 onion, sliced

1 stalk celery, diced

1 whole fresh Anaheim pepper

2 whole cloves

3 sprigs parsley

2 bay leaves

1 teaspoon salt, plus more to taste

1 teaspoon black pepper, plus more
   to taste

1/4 teaspoon dried thyme

1 carrot, cut into 1/2-inch slices (optional)

2 pounds fish (bass, catfish, cod, orange
   roughy, salmon, tuna, sole, trout, or
   flounder), cut into 1-inch-thick fillets.

3 tablespoons cornstarch

1. Put all the ingredients except the fish and the cornstarch in a large saucepan. Bring to a boil and simmer, uncovered, 30 minutes. Strain the court bouillon, reserving the vegetables in a separate bowl and discarding the cloves, bay leaves, and Anaheim pepper.

2. Pour the court bouillon back into the saucepan and heat to a simmer. Put the fish fillets in the court bouillon, cover, and simmer gently over low heat about 10 minutes. Using a slotted spatula, remove the fish to a platter and cover loosely with a piece of foil to keep warm. Pour the liquid in a blender or a food processor along with the reserved vegetables. Add the cornstarch and puree until thick and smooth. Serve alongside the fish.

Papaya Shrimp with Sautéed Garlic

YIELD: 4 SERVINGS

This creamy dish has a delightful flavor and looks elegant when served with the seasoned papaya strips.

8 tablespoons (1 stick) butter
2 cloves garlic, minced
1 stalk celery, diced
1 medium onion, diced
1/2 cup water
1/2 cup white wine vinegar
2 tablespoons sugar
1 bay leaf
4 cups shrimp stock or chicken broth

2 cups heavy cream
24 large shrimp, shelled and deveined
1 teaspoon salt
1 teaspoon black pepper
2 small, ripe papayas, peeled, seeded, and cut into strips
1 teaspoon dried thyme
1 teaspoon dried basil

1. In a large saucepan over low heat, melt 4 tablespoons butter. Add the garlic and sauté until lightly browned, about 10 minutes. Add the celery and onion and cook until the onion is soft and transparent. Add 1/2 cup water, the vinegar, sugar, bay leaf, and stock. Increase the heat to high and cook until the liquid is reduced by half, about 8 to 10 minutes; remove from heat. Stir in the cream.

2. In a skillet, melt the remaining 4 tablespoons butter. Add the shrimp and cook until slightly pink, 2 or 3 minutes. Add the salt and pepper.

3. In a medium bowl, toss the papaya strips with the thyme and basil. Spoon the sauce onto 4 dinner plates, set strips of papaya in the center of each, and surround with 6 cooked shrimp per serving.

Grilled Fish with Spicy Marinade

YIELD: 6 SERVINGS

A fish trap doesn't make any noise, but it does good work. —Slave proverb

1 teaspoon dried tarragon

1 teaspoon dried basil

1 teaspoon dried thyme

1 teaspoon hot paprika

1 teaspoon dried oregano

1 teaspoon fennel seed

1 teaspoon anise seed

2 tablespoons fresh lemon juice

2 tablespoons fresh lime juice

1 tablespoon white wine vinegar

2 tablespoons Worcestershire sauce

1/2 Scotch bonnet or jalapeño pepper, minced

2 cups vegetable oil

6 fillets mild, light-fleshed fish such as flounder, bass, or catfish (about 4 ounces each)

1. In a shallow bowl, combine all the ingredients except the fish. Add the fish and coat each piece thoroughly with the marinade. Refrigerate for at least 1 hour.

2. Remove the rack from the grill and oil it with vegetable oil. Start the charcoal for the grill. Allow the coals to become partly white with ash before cooking the fish. Place the marinated fish on the grill, turning once when the flesh becomes opaque, about 3 minutes. Do not overcook.

Also pictured: Orange Rice (page 98)

Swordfish with Tomatillo Sauce

YIELD: 4 SERVINGS

Tomatillos look like green, husk-covered tomatoes. You can find them fresh or canned in many supermarkets. They make a wonderful sauce for baked or broiled fish, and this tomatillo sauce can also be used as a dip.

4 swordfish steaks, about 3/4 inch thick
   (about 2 pounds)
2 tablespoons fresh lemon juice

TOMATILLO SAUCE:
1/2 pound fresh tomatillos, husks removed
   and quartered, or 1 (11-ounce) can
   tomatillos, drained and quartered

1 large tomato, chopped
1/2 cup chopped cilantro
1/2 small red bell pepper, seeded and
   chopped
1/2 cup white vinegar
1 teaspoon salt
1/2 Scotch bonnet pepper, forced through
   a garlic press or finely minced

1. Start the charcoal for the grill or preheat the broiler. If you are grilling the fish, remove the rack from the grill and oil it with vegetable oil. Sprinkle the swordfish with the lemon juice, cover, and set aside.

2. To prepare the sauce: Combine all the ingredients except the Scotch bonnet pepper in a blender or food processor until fine, but not liquefied (some solids should remain). If it is too thick, add a little more vinegar. Mix in half of the crushed Scotch bonnet pepper. This pepper is very hot, and it takes about 15 minutes for its flavor to seep through the other ingredients. It is best to wait for 15 minutes and taste the sauce again before adding any additional pepper.

3. When the coals are partly white with ash, grill (or broil) the swordfish 3 minutes per side, or until it is still slightly pink in the center.

4. Sprinkle the fish with salt and pepper and serve immediately with the tomatillo sauce.

Meals

Chicken with Coconut Sauce

YIELD: 4 SERVINGS

> When the preacher comes by for Sunday dinner, it makes the chickens cry. —Slave proverb

2 cups all-purpose flour
1 teaspoon salt
1 teaspoon black pepper
1 teaspoon sweet paprika
1/2 teaspoon cayenne pepper
1 (2-1/2 pound) fryer chicken, quartered
1/4 cup vegetable oil
1 medium onion, sliced

1 green bell pepper, seeded and sliced
1 medium tomato, peeled and sliced
1/2 teaspoon curry powder
1/4 teaspoon ground saffron
11/2 cups chicken broth
3 tablespoons unsweetened grated coconut

1. In a large resealable plastic bag, combine the flour, salt, black pepper, paprika, and cayenne pepper. Drop in the chicken pieces and shake until well coated.

2. In a heavy skillet over high heat, heat the oil until hot but not smoking. Reduce the heat to low, add the onion, bell pepper, and tomato, and cook until the vegetables are wilted and tender, about 8 minutes. Remove the vegetables from the skillet with a slotted spoon and set aside. Add the chicken to the skillet and sprinkle it with the curry powder and saffron.

3. Cook the chicken 15 minutes over low heat, turning occasionally, until lightly browned. Return the vegetables to the skillet, cover, and continue cooking over low heat until the chicken is tender, about 20 minutes.

4. While the chicken is cooking, heat the broth over medium-high heat in a small saucepan. Add the coconut and simmer about 10 minutes. Strain into a small bowl, then pour the liquid over the chicken. Stir well. Cover and continue to simmer the chicken and vegetables until the seasonings are well blended, about 10 minutes.

Jerk Pork

YIELD: 8 SERVINGS

Jerk is the Caribbean method of marinating meats before barbecuing. The technique for making jerk was created by the Arawaks, the first settlers of the Caribbean Islands, and developed into a mouthwatering Island tradition by the Maroons, runaway slaves whose guerrilla tactics against Caribbean slave owners eventually won them their freedom. The combined methods of spicing and smoking the meat preserved it in the remote places where the Maroons took refuge. The vegetables and spices used in jerk can easily be found in the wild on the Islands and in our own (tamer) grocery stores. Jerk is one of the most popular dishes in Jamaica, and jerk "cook shacks" dot the island like palm trees. This marinade is also delicious when used for chicken.

1/4 cup ground allspice

7 scallions, chopped

1/2 Scotch bonnet or jalapeño pepper

2 cloves garlic

Leaves from 4 sprigs fresh thyme or 1
   tablespoon dried

5 bay leaves

1 teaspoon salt

1 teaspoon black pepper

1 tablespoon vegetable oil, as needed

5 pounds thick-cut pork loin chops

1. Place all the ingredients except the oil and the pork in a blender or food processor. Grind the spices to a paste, adding vegetable oil if necessary. Rinse the pork, pat dry, and put it in a pan. Coat it with the jerk paste. Cover the pan with plastic wrap, refrigerate, and marinate for at least 1 hour. Jerk is best when it has marinated overnight in the refrigerator.

2. Make a fire in the grill and allow the coals to become partly white with ash before cooking the pork. If desired, place sprigs of thyme or bay leaves on the coals for added flavor. Place the marinated meat on the grill. Cook about 5 minutes, turning once. Cook until done, another 5 minutes.

Also pictured: Twice-Baked Sweet Potatoes (page 104)

Griots

YIELD: 4 SERVINGS

Many West African storytellers and historians are called griots. I don't know how this dish got its name, but I like to think it might have been served as a reward for a wonderful evening of stories. These flavorful cubes of pork are popular treats in Haiti and are often served with mashed plantains, sliced avocados, and watercress.

1 cup chopped onion

1/4 cup chopped shallots or chives

1 cup orange juice

1/4 cup fresh lime juice

1/4 cup water

1/8 teaspoon dried thyme

1/2 teaspoon salt

1/2 teaspoon black pepper

2 pounds boneless pork, cut into 2-inch cubes

2 tablespoons vegetable oil

1. Put all the ingredients except the oil and the pork in a bowl and mix well. Add the pork and toss until well coated. Marinate in the refrigerator for at least 4 hours. Drain off the marinade and set it aside.

2. In a frying pan, heat the oil over high heat until hot but not smoking; brown the pork on all sides. Add the marinade and cover; reduce the heat to low. Simmer 30 minutes. Uncover and increase the heat to medium. Cook until the liquids have evaporated, 8 to 10 minutes.

Papaya Beef

YIELD: 6 SERVINGS

This recipe has been used since the time of slavery. Most of the meat on a plantation went to the owners; slaves seldom ate meat, and when they did, it was usually the toughest cuts. Innovative slave cooks found a way to tenderize the meat by using slices of papaya, which contains the enzyme papain, a natural tenderizer.

1 large ripe papaya, peeled and sliced,
   seeds removed and retained
3 pounds round steak, cut into 6 steaks
1 tablespoon olive oil
1 medium yellow onion, sliced

1 teaspoon salt
1 teaspoon black pepper
1 tablespoon Worcestershire sauce
1 large tomato, peeled and chopped
1 (16-ounce) can lentils

1. Lay half the sliced papaya on the bottom of a large glass or ceramic pan (metal may react with the papaya). Cover the papaya with the steaks. Lay the rest of the papaya slices on top. Cover the dish and refrigerate 2 to 3 hours.

2. Preheat the oven to 325 degrees. Spread the oil in the bottom of a glass baking pan or an enameled casserole. Layer the onion slices on top of the oil. Remove the steaks from the refrigerator and season with the salt, pepper, and Worcestershire sauce. Lay the steaks over the onion and cover with the papaya and the tomato. Tightly cover the baking pan or casserole and bake until the meat is tender, about 30 minutes. Remove the dish from the oven and spread the lentils and papaya seeds over the meat. Return the dish to the oven and bake, uncovered, 10 minutes longer.

Sunset Jazz Spicy Spareribs

YIELD: 4 SERVINGS

This succulent recipe is my tribute to St. Croix's Blue Moon Café's barbecue ribs. The Sunset Jazz Festival is a monthly event on St. Croix and many of the other restaurants in the area prepare a special menu. There's nothing better than good food and good jazz music with a backdrop of some of the most beautiful sunsets and ocean scenery you'll probably ever see. This is one of my favorite ways to prepare pork ribs to ensure that they will be tender but full of spicy flavor. The brown sugar, vinegar, soy sauce, and pineapple give the meat a tangy, delicious taste, and the ginger and hot sauce add just the right touch of spiciness. Frequent basting keeps the meat moist and tender.

1 (2-pound) slab St. Louis–style pork ribs
3/4 cup packed brown sugar
1/4 cup white vinegar
2 tablespoons soy sauce
11/2 teaspoons salt
11/2 teaspoons black pepper

1 teaspoon paprika
1 teaspoon ground ginger
1 (14-ounce) can crushed pineapple
   with juice
2 tablespoons Tabasco sauce

1. Cut the slab into individual ribs and put the pieces in a large pot. Cover the ribs with water and simmer 20 minutes. Drain off the water and put the ribs in a baking pan.

2. In a small saucepan, combine the brown sugar, vinegar, soy sauce, salt, black pepper, paprika, and ginger. Bring to a boil. Add the pineapple with juice. Reduce the heat and simmer the mixture for 5 minutes. Remove from the heat and stir in the Tabasco sauce. You may want to add more brown sugar if you like a sweeter sauce, or more Tabasco sauce, if you prefer a spicier version.

3. Brush each rib with the sauce. Heat the broiler and broil about 5 to 7 minutes on each side or until done, basting often.

Also pictured: Rice Salad (page 71)

Eggs, Vegetables, and Side Dishes

Ackee and Scrambled Eggs

YIELD: 4 SERVINGS

Ackee is extremely popular in Jamaica and relatively unknown in other parts of the world, except as a specialty item sold in cans. Ackee trees were brought along as cargo to the Caribbean Islands during the days of the slave trade. Legend has it that slaves familiar with the uses of ackee poisoned their masters with the deadly red, unripened fruit. Ackee is ripe when it has burst open, showing the yellow, edible fruit inside. The look and texture of ackee is similar to scrambled eggs which is why the ingredients blend together so well.

4 large eggs

1 cup canned ackee, drained

1/2 teaspoon chopped cilantro

2 tablespoons half-and-half or cream

1 teaspoon salt

1 teaspoon black pepper

3 tablespoons butter

1. In a medium bowl, beat together until foamy all the ingredients except the butter. In a skillet over medium-high heat, melt the butter. Pour the egg mixture into the skillet, scraping the bottom and sides constantly with a spoon. Remove the skillet from the heat as soon as the eggs have partly set, about 3 minutes. Continue to stir. Serve as soon as the eggs are cooked but are still fluffy.

Puerto Rican Piñon

YIELD: 6 SERVINGS

There's a large Puerto Rican population in the U.S. Virgin Islands and their cultural influence there is evident. Piñon, a great dish for breakfast or brunch, will taste even better if you have an audience to watch you prepare it. The trick is to flip the egg and meat mixture out of the pan onto a curved pot lid. Then you slide the piñon back into the pan again on top of another layer of eggs. It sounds (and looks) harder than it is. Who knows, your guests may be so impressed they'll even volunteer to do the dishes!

1 pound pork sausage or chorizo, crumbled
4 ripe plantains (skin should be almost black), peeled and sliced lengthwise
6 eggs
1 tablespoon prepared salsa
1 teaspoon salt
1 teaspoon black pepper
3 tablespoons vegetable oil
1/2 cup shredded Monterey Jack cheese

1. In a skillet over high heat, fry the sausage or chorizo until brown. Remove the meat from the skillet with a slotted spoon. Fry the plantains in the oil remaining in the pan until golden brown. Remove the fried plantains.

2. In a bowl, beat together the eggs, salsa, salt, and black pepper. In a clean nonstick skillet over medium-high heat, heat the oil until hot but not smoking. Pour half the egg mixture into the pan. Do not stir. Working quickly, layer half the plantain slices over the eggs, spread the meat over the plantain, and top with the remaining plantain slices. Cook over low to moderate heat until the eggs are firm, about 3 minutes. Take a pot lid and invert the contents onto the underside of the lid. Add enough oil to the pan to cook the remaining egg mixture and pour it into the pan. Slide the piñon back off the pot lid into the pan on top of the raw eggs (the cooked eggs remain on top). Cook until the eggs on the bottom are done, about 3 minutes. Sprinkle with the cheese and serve immediately.

Calypso Corn and Black Bean Salad

YIELD: 6 SERVINGS

I love the festive colors in this dish. It's one of my favorite dishes to serve at a summer party.

2 cups fresh corn, or 1 (10-ounce) package frozen corn kernels, thawed
2 (15-ounce) cans black beans, drained and rinsed
1 large red bell pepper, stemmed, seeded, and diced
1 small fresh jalapeño chile, stemmed, seeded, and minced
1/2 cup firmly packed chopped fresh cilantro
1/4 cup fresh lime juice
2 tablespoons vegetable oil
1 teaspoon sugar
1 teaspoon salt
1 teaspoon black pepper

1. Combine all the ingredients in a large bowl. Taste and adjust seasonings. Cover and chill 1 hour or overnight to combine flavors.

Concombre en Daube (Stewed Cucumbers)

YIELD: 6 SERVINGS

This unusual recipe is the solution for a garden that has produced far more cucumbers than you can pickle or eat in salads.

3 tablespoons olive oil or vegetable oil
1 onion, chopped
3 tomatoes, peeled and chopped
1 teaspoon salt
1 teaspoon black pepper
1/4 teaspoon sugar
3 medium cucumbers, peeled, halved lengthwise, seeded, and thickly sliced

1. In a medium saucepan, heat the oil until hot but not smoking and sauté the onion until golden and tender. Add the tomatoes, salt, black pepper, and sugar. Stir in the cucumbers. Cover the saucepan and simmer over low heat 45 minutes. Place in a sealed container and refrigerate.

Coo Coo

YIELD: 8 TO 10 SLICES

The history of this recipe can be traced to the indians of Brazil. No one really knows how coo coo spread to the Islands, although its preparation is very similar to that of the African mealie meal recipe. Coo coo is usually served as a starchy vegetable side dish, with meat or fish as the main course. Coo coo is called fungi in the Caribbean and can be made without the okra. It is similar in texture to polenta and an example of the way that African slave cooks influenced the cuisine of the Caribbean.

3 cups water

1 teaspoon salt

8 small okra, washed, stemmed, and
   sliced crosswise

1 cup cornmeal

1 tablespoon butter

1. In a heavy saucepan, bring 3 cups water to a boil. Add the salt and okra. Cover, reduce heat to low, and cook about 10 minutes. Drain the okra, reserving the cooking water. Set the okra aside.

2. Return 1 1/2 cups of the cooking water to the saucepan and bring it to a boil. Rapidly stir in the cornmeal in a steady stream to form a stiff paste. Stir until the mixture is smooth. Gradually add about 1/2 cup more of the cooking water, cover, and cook over low heat about 5 minutes. Butter a mold or loaf pan.

3. Stir in the cooked okra, adding more water if necessary to make the coo coo smooth. Continue to cook slowly, stirring occasionally, until the mixture is stiff, about 5 minutes. Scrape the coo coo into the mold or loaf pan, let it set for 1 hour, and turn it out onto a plate. Slice before serving.

Creole-Style Green Beans

YIELD: 8 SERVINGS

"I would never be of any service to anyone as a slave." —Nat Turner

1 (10-ounce) package frozen French-style
  green beans
2 tablespoons vegetable oil
2 stalks celery, diced
1 green bell pepper, seeds and membrane
  removed, diced

1 small onion, diced
1 (28-ounce) can tomatoes, drained and
  coarsely chopped
1/2 teaspoon sugar
1/8 teaspoon salt
1/8 teaspoon black pepper

1. Cook green beans according to package directions and set aside.

2. Heat the oil in a large skillet over medium-high heat. Sauté the celery, bell pepper, and onion until tender, about 5 minutes. Add the tomatoes and simmer uncovered 15 minutes or until most of the liquid has evaporated. Add the sugar, salt, black pepper, and green beans to the skillet. Simmer 5 minutes.

Orange Rice

YIELD: 8 SERVINGS

The orange juice and the zest provide a bright burst of citrus flavor to this rice dish. It's a fantastic accompaniment to grilled fish.

2 cups fresh orange juice
1 tablespoon butter
1 tablespoon sugar

1 cup uncooked rice
2 tablespoons grated orange zest

1. In a medium saucepan, bring the orange juice to a boil. Stir in the butter, sugar, and rice, combining well, then cover tightly. Simmer the rice over low heat, about 18 minutes. Do not lift the cover or stir.

2. Remove the pan from the heat. Add the orange zest and stir. The rice should be tender and the liquid absorbed.

Metagee

YIELD: 8 SERVINGS

This recipe has as many names and variations as the variety of vegetables it contains. Metagee is also called sancoche, sancocho, oildown, and oileen. A top layer of cooked fish or dumplings is sometimes added. I prefer this vegetarian version for the flavor that results when all the different vegetables blend with the coconut milk and cook down to creamy perfection. You can vary the vegetables, as long as the firmer root vegetables stay on the bottom and the more tender vegetables are layered on top.

2 green plantains, peeled

1 1/2 pounds cocoyams or white potatoes, peeled

1 1/2 pounds sweet potatoes, peeled

2 large carrots, peeled

1/2 pound pumpkin, peeled, seeded, and membrane removed

1 large onion, sliced

6 to 8 okra, ends and stems removed

1 teaspoon dried thyme

1 teaspoon salt

1 teaspoon black pepper

3 cups coconut milk

1. Cut the peeled vegetables into large pieces. In a heavy covered pot or Dutch oven, layer the vegetables: start with the plantains, then the cocoyams or white potatoes, the sweet potatoes, carrots, pumpkin, onion, and okra.

2. Combine the thyme, salt, and black pepper with the coconut milk. Pour half the coconut milk mixture down the sides of the pot containing the vegetables and the rest over the top. Over high heat, bring the vegetables to a boil. Cover, reduce the heat, and simmer until some of the liquid has evaporated and the vegetables on the bottom are fork-tender, about 30 minutes.

Spicy Coconutty Rice

YIELD: 6 SERVINGS

The United Caribbean Association (UCA) is a combination community center and restaurant in St. Croix in the U.S. Virgin Islands. It serves a delicious menu composed of Rastafarian and vegetarian recipes ranging from smoothies and drinks made from maubee bark, lemon grass, tofu, or chlorophyll to a spicy popcorn infused with B12 nutritional yeast to boost the health component of the snack. I loved their veggie basket, which is full of crisp, batter-fried slices of pumpkin, cauliflower, broccoli, and carrots. This is my variation of their wonderful recipe for spicy coconutty rice.

1 tablespoon olive oil
1 onion, chopped
2 cloves garlic, chopped
1/2 cup seeded and diced green jalapeño or Anaheim chiles
2 teaspoons salt
1 teaspoon black pepper
1 teaspoon ground cumin

1 1/2 cups uncooked long-grain rice
1/4 cup coconut milk
3 cups water
2 tablespoons unsweetened coconut flakes
2 tablespoons chopped fresh cilantro
1/2 teaspoon grated lime zest

1. In a heavy saucepan over medium-high heat, heat the oil until hot but not smoking. Add the onion, garlic, chiles, salt, black pepper, and cumin and cook over low heat until the onion turns translucent, about 5 minutes. Add the rice, and mix until evenly coated; cook for 1 minute. Add the coconut milk and 3 cups water. Stir well and bring to a boil. Cover the pot, turn the heat to low, and simmer slowly for 15 minutes.

2. Remove the pot from the heat. Fluff the rice with a fork and add the coconut flakes, cilantro, and lime zest.

Magic Kitchen Potato Stuffing

YIELD: 8 SERVINGS

Anastasia Rivers is the owner and chef of the Magic Kitchen on the island of St. Croix, in the U.S. Virgin Islands. I spent a wonderful afternoon learning how to prepare some of their fabulous recipes. This potato stuffing recipe is my version of the delicious dish that Anastasia makes for her customers. It's great as a side dish or as a stuffing for chicken or whole fish.

6 large white potatoes, peeled and diced

1 teaspoon salt

5 tablespoons butter, plus more for greasing dish

1/4 cup evaporated milk

1/4 cup whole milk

2 tablespoons brown sugar

2 tablespoons ketchup

1 tablespoon tomato paste

1 large yellow onion, minced

1 large red bell pepper, minced

1/2 habanero pepper, minced, seeds and membranes removed

1 teaspoon dried thyme

1/2 teaspoon cinnamon

1/2 cup raisins

1 egg, beaten

1. Preheat the oven to 350 degrees. Put the potatoes in a large saucepan or pot and cover with water; add the salt. Bring to a boil, then reduce the heat and simmer until the potatoes are soft, about 20 minutes. Drain the potatoes.

2. Using a potato ricer or masher, gently mash the potatoes until the texture is fluffy. Stir in 4 tablespoons butter, the evaporated and whole milk, brown sugar, ketchup, and tomato paste. Set the potatoes aside.

3. In a small skillet, melt the remaining 1 tablespoon butter over medium heat; sauté the onion, bell pepper, and habanero pepper until tender, 3 to 5 minutes.

4. Stir in the thyme, cinnamon, and the raisins and continue to cook the mixture another 2 to 3 minutes. Gently combine the egg and the vegetable mixture with the potato mixture. Lightly butter a baking dish. Spoon the potato stuffing into the baking dish and bake 20 to 25 minutes, until the top of the stuffing is golden brown.

Pigeon Peas and Rice

YIELD: 8 SERVINGS

This dish is as important to island cuisine as palm trees and beaches are to island scenery.

1 1/2 cups dried pigeon peas, picked over
1/4 pound salt pork, diced
2 onions, chopped
1 stalk celery, chopped
1/2 cup chopped green bell pepper
1 clove garlic, chopped
6 cups water

1 teaspoon salt
1 teaspoon black pepper
1/2 teaspoon cayenne pepper
1/2 teaspoon dried thyme
2 sprigs parsley, chopped
2 cups uncooked long-grain rice

1. Put the peas in a pot, cover with cold water, and bring to a rapid boil. Remove from the heat and set aside for 1 hour. Drain and rinse the peas.

2. In a Dutch oven or heavy skillet, sauté the salt pork over medium-high heat until golden. Remove with a slotted spoon and set aside. Add the onion, celery, bell pepper, and garlic to the skillet. Cook the vegetables over low heat until tender. Return the salt pork to the skillet and add the peas, 6 cups water, salt, black pepper, cayenne pepper, thyme, and parsley. Bring to a boil, then reduce the heat and simmer until the peas are tender, about 40 minutes.

3. Add the rice and stir. Cover the skillet and simmer over low heat until all the liquid is absorbed and the rice is tender, about 30 minutes.

Spinach Fritters

YIELD: 4 SERVINGS

Them that eats can say grace. —Slave proverb

1 pound spinach, washed and stems
  removed
4 tablespoons (1/2 stick) butter
1 teaspoon dried thyme
1 teaspoon dried marjoram
2 tablespoons minced onion

1 teaspoon black pepper
1 teaspoon salt
1/2 green bell pepper, seeded and diced
1 egg, lightly beaten
1/2 cup bread crumbs
2 cups vegetable oil

1. Place the slightly wet spinach in a pot. Add the butter, thyme, marjoram, minced onion, black pepper, and salt. Over low heat, cook the spinach in its own moisture until tender, about 10 minutes.

2. Drain off the excess liquid and chop the spinach finely, then add the bell pepper and the egg. Stir in enough bread crumbs to make a firm consistency. Form into 8 to 10 balls.

3. In a deep skillet, heat the oil over high heat until hot but not smoking; fry the spinach fritters until brown, about 3 minutes, flipping halfway through. Drain on paper towels.

Twice-Baked Sweet Potatoes

YIELD: 8 SERVINGS

When one is very hungry, one doesn't peel the sweet potato. —Caribbean proverb

4 medium sweet potatoes
1/2 cup milk
1/4 cup smooth peanut butter
1/4 teaspoon ground cinnamon

1/2 teaspoon salt
1/2 teaspoon ground nutmeg
1/2 cup chopped peanuts

1. Preheat the oven to 425 degrees. Arrange the sweet potatoes on a cookie sheet or in a baking pan. Bake until fork-tender, 50 to 60 minutes. Lower the oven heat to 350 degrees. (If using a microwave, arrange the sweet potatoes like the spokes of a wheel with the smaller ends in the middle. Microwave on high 10 to 15 minutes, or until fork-tender.)

2. When the sweet potatoes are cool enough to handle, slice each one lengthwise. Leaving the shells intact, scoop out the flesh and put it in a bowl. Mash the flesh, then add the milk, peanut butter, cinnamon, and salt and beat until fluffy. Spoon back into the shells. Sprinkle with the nutmeg and peanuts and place on a baking sheet.

3. Bake the sweet potatoes until lightly browned, about 10 minutes. (If using a microwave oven, microwave on medium for 4 minutes.)

Breads and Desserts

Baked Banana Custard

YIELD: 8 SERVINGS

This dessert is easy to prepare and light enough to serve after a substantial meal.

4 ripe bananas

5 tablespoons sugar

1/4 teaspoon ground nutmeg, plus more
    for topping the custard

Juice of 1 lime

2 tablespoons butter

1/2 cup bread crumbs

3 eggs

2 cups milk

1. Preheat the oven to 325 degrees. Peel the bananas, removing the threads, and mash until fairly smooth. Add 2 tablespoons sugar, the nutmeg, and the lime juice and mix well. Butter a 9x13-inch baking dish. Spread the banana mixture evenly in the dish. Cover the bananas with the bread crumbs.

2. Beat the eggs, gradually beating in the remaining 3 tablespoons sugar. Heat the milk over medium-high heat until warm; do not boil. Slowly add the milk to the beaten eggs to temper them, stirring until well blended. Pour the egg mixture over the bananas and sprinkle with nutmeg. Bake until the custard is set, 20 to 25 minutes. Refrigerate and serve cold.

Key Lime Pie

YIELD: ONE 9-INCH PIE

Key lime pie is one of the most popular desserts on the Islands. Authentic key lime pie has a yellow filling and a pastry crust. The round, beige key limes are common in the Caribbean and Florida but are more difficult to find in other parts of the United States; however, bottled key lime juice may be available. Although the flavor won't be as acidic, you can substitute the juice from green limes.

1 (9-inch) pie crust (page 250)
3 jumbo or 4 large eggs, separated
1 (14-ounce) can sweetened condensed
    milk
1/2 cup fresh key lime or green lime juice,
    or 1/2 cup bottled key lime juice

1/2 teaspoon cream of tartar
1/8 teaspoon salt
4 tablespoons sugar
1/2 teaspoon vanilla extract

1. Preheat the oven to 425 degrees. Prick the piecrust on the bottom and sides with a fork. Bake the piecrust until it is a light golden brown, about 10 minutes, and set aside to cool.

2. Reset the oven to 325 degrees. In a medium bowl, and using an electric mixer set on medium speed, beat the egg yolks until thick. Add the condensed milk to the beaten yolks and beat until well blended. Add the lime juice and beat again for 2 minutes. Set aside.

3. In a small bowl, with the electric mixer set on moderate speed, beat the egg whites until frothy. Blend in the cream of tartar and salt. Add the sugar 1 tablespoon at a time. Add the vanilla and beat on high speed until the meringue is glossy and stands in soft peaks when the beaters are withdrawn. Do not overbeat. Add a quarter of the meringue to the filling and combine well.

4. Pour the filling into the baked piecrust. Spoon the remaining meringue over the top of the pie, spreading it so that it completely covers the filling and the edges. Bake the pie until the meringue is golden brown, about 15 minutes. Let the pie cool for 2 hours before refrigerating; serve chilled.

Bakes

YIELD: ABOUT 2 DOZEN

These crisp fried biscuits traveled from the Islands to America along with slave cooks. Bakes became fried biscuits and were cooked in the grease that was left after fixing a batch of Southern fried chicken.

2 cups all-purpose flour
2 teaspoons baking powder
1/2 teaspoon salt
2 teaspoons sugar

2 tablespoons shortening
1/4 cup cold water
1/2 cup vegetable oil

1. In a large mixing bowl, sift together the flour, baking powder, salt, and sugar. With a pastry cutter or fork, cut in the shortening; the mixture should be crumbly. Add the water a little at a time, mixing by hand until a soft dough forms. Knead the dough lightly on a floured board, adding a little more flour if it is too sticky. Pinch off walnut-sized pieces of dough and roll them into balls.

2. Flatten the balls into circles about 1/2 inch thick. In a heavy skillet, heat the oil over medium-high heat until hot but not smoking and fry the bakes until golden brown on both sides, about 3 to 5 minutes.

Orange Bread

YIELD: ONE 9X5-INCH LOAF

This citrus-flavored bread is superb sliced, toasted, and buttered.

4 tablespoons (1/2 stick) unsalted butter,
    melted, plus more for pan
2 cups all-purpose flour
4 teaspoons baking powder
1/2 cup sugar

1/2 teaspoon salt
1 tablespoon grated orange zest
1 egg, well beaten
1 cup orange juice

1. Preheat the oven to 350 degrees. Grease a 9x5-inch loaf pan. Sift together the flour, baking powder, sugar, salt, and orange zest.

2. Combine the egg with the orange juice and butter and stir slowly into the flour. Pour the batter into the prepared pan and bake 30 minutes, or until a cake tester comes out clean.

Matrimony

YIELD: 6 SERVINGS

This is a perfect dessert for a wedding dinner. Starfruit, also called carambola, was once pretty exotic. Now it can be found in most grocery stores. Choose full, firm, yellow fruit with thick, wide ribs to ensure that you're buying the sweetest ones. Starfruit with narrow ribs are as sour as lemons. The starfruit and the oranges in this dessert make a lovely pairing.

6 large starfruit
4 oranges
1 (14-ounce) can sweetened condensed
    milk
Ground nutmeg

1. Halve each starfruit; the cross sections of the fruit will be star-shaped. The pulp of the starfruit is very soft and full of seeds. Scoop it out with a spoon and pick out the seeds. Peel and section the oranges. Combine the starfruit pulp and the orange sections, then refrigerate. When you are ready to serve, stir in the condensed milk. Place the hollowed starfruit in the center of the plate and the orange-starfruit mixture around it. Sprinkle with the nutmeg.

Pineapple Rice Pudding

YIELD: 6 SERVINGS

This is an elegant version of the traditional Spanish rice pudding (arroz con leche). The fluffy meringue and pineapple-flavored sauce add a Caribbean touch.

2 tablespoons butter, plus more for pan
2 cups cooked rice
3 cups milk
1/3 cup plus 2 tablespoons granulated sugar
1/2 teaspoon salt, plus a pinch
3 eggs, separated

1 1/2 teaspoons vanilla extract
1 (20-ounce) can crushed pineapple, with juice reserved
1/2 cup flaked, sweetened coconut
1 tablespoon cornstarch
1/4 cup packed brown sugar

1. Preheat the oven to 325 degrees. Butter a 9x13-inch baking dish. In a medium saucepan, combine the rice, 2 1/2 cups of the milk, 1/3 cup sugar, 1 tablespoon butter, and 1/2 teaspoon salt. Over medium heat, stir until thick and creamy, about 20 minutes. Beat the egg yolks with the remaining 1/2 cup milk. Add to the rice mixture, cook about 1 minute, and remove from the heat. Stir in 1 teaspoon of the vanilla extract and the pineapple. Refrigerate until cool.

2. In a small mixing bowl, beat the egg whites until foamy. Gradually add the remaining 2 tablespoons sugar, beating until the whites hold stiff peaks but are not dry. Fold the meringue into the cooled rice mixture and turn into the buttered baking dish. Sprinkle with the coconut. Bake 20 to 25 minutes.

3. In a medium saucepan over low heat, mix the reserved pineapple juice with the cornstarch. Stir until the cornstarch is completely dissolved. Add the remaining 1 tablespoon butter, the brown sugar, and the pinch of salt. Cook, stirring frequently, until clear and thickened. Add the remaining 1/2 teaspoon vanilla extract. Just before serving, drizzle the sauce over the warm pudding.

Drinks

Barley Lemonade

YIELD 6 TO 8 SERVINGS

3 quarts plus 1 cup water
1/2 cup barley
2 cups sugar

Grated zest of 1 lemon
2 lemons, peeled, sectioned, and seeded

1. In a small saucepan, combine 3 quarts water and the barley. Over low heat, simmer until the water has been reduced by about a third, 20 to 30 minutes. Pour through a fine sieve into a gallon pitcher. Discard barley.

2. In a small saucepan, combine the sugar, the remaining 1 cup water, the zest, and the lemon pulp and boil until it makes a slightly thick simple syrup. Push the lemon mixture through a sieve, discarding the pulp that remains. Stir the lemon mixture into the barley water. Refrigerate and serve over ice.

Naranjada (Orange Cocktail)

YIELD: 4 SERVINGS

Juice of 4 oranges
1/4 cup sugar
1 1/2 cups sparkling mineral water or
    club soda
2 cups crushed ice

1. Pour the orange juice into a 2-quart pitcher. Add the sugar and stir to mix well. Add the mineral water or club soda and the crushed ice. Chill.

Peanut and Banana Punch

YIELD: 4 SERVINGS

2 cups whole milk
5 tablespoons sweetened condensed milk
1/2 banana
3 tablespoons smooth peanut butter

1/4 teaspoon ground cinnamon
1/4 teaspoon vanilla extract
3 cups crushed ice

1. Put all the ingredients except the ice in a blender; liquefy and serve immediately over the crushed ice.

Nectar Punch

YIELD: 4 SERVINGS

1 (11½-ounce) can banana nectar
1 (11½-ounce) can apricot nectar

Juice of 1 lime
2 cups club soda

1. Combine all the ingredients in a large pitcher and refrigerate.

Refresco de Coco y Piña (Coconut and Pineapple Drink)

YIELD: 3 TO 4 SERVINGS

2 cups coconut milk
2½ cups canned crushed pineapple,
   drained

2 tablespoons sugar
1/8 teaspoon almond extract

1. In a blender, combine all the ingredients. Blend at high speed until the mixture is smooth. Strain through a fine sieve into a pitcher. Refrigerate until thoroughly chilled. Serve over ice.

Making Do
Slave Kitchens

Aunt Jemima and Me

Like many Americans, I've grown up with the image of Aunt Jemima, the smiling, bandana-wearing, rotund African-American woman depicted as the perfect cook on the pancake box. When I was younger, Aunt Jemima was a source of embarrassment. She was also a vivid reminder of slavery, and of the mammy that was forced to cook and clean for the master and his family. She was the one taking care of other peoples' families while her own loved ones fended for themselves.

Aunt Jemima was also the pictorial example of everything that was supposedly unattractive about African-American women. She was large, she was dark, her hair curly and coarse, and her facial features weren't the acceptable example of what was supposedly considered beautiful. Aunt Jemima looked a lot like me and many of the women I knew. As I've grown to love what I look like, I've also grown to love Aunt Jemima.

As a child, I was embarrassed by the cast iron Aunt Jemima statues and mammy dolls. Now I have a small collection of those figurines and dolls in my kitchen. Some are from the Caribbean and others are from the American South, but they all represent a woman who overcame, created, persevered, and triumphed in the face of obstacles that would have destroyed a lesser being.

I know from studying history that African-American women are the foundation of American life as we know it. We worked side by side with African-American men to till the fields, we cooked the food, raised children, and held our families together in good times and in bad. We upheld our faith in God, and instilled that faith in our children. We prayed for deliverance and marched for freedom. We never gave up on our belief that tomorrow would be a better day for our people and worked tirelessly to make those dreams come true.

For hundreds of years, legions of anonymous Aunt Jemimas performed culinary miracles to turn scraps, offal, remnants, and bones into recipes that are now served in the finest five-star restaurants. The recipes in this section are a tribute to the ingenuity of my ancestors, both women and men, who "made do" with what they had and made it taste delicious.

As a writer, historian, and cook, I often think about the many accomplishments of the African captives who were enslaved in America. Many of their innovative creations have gone unrecognized in history. When I began researching this section of The New African-American Kitchen, I discovered a large group of women and men whose expertise greatly enhanced American cooking, but whose contributions are seldom noted in cookbooks because they were slaves. These African and African-American cooks concocted dishes that became mainstays in the South and spread across America. They devised ingenious substitutions for ingredients from their homelands that could not be found in America. The real genius of the slave cooks, however, lay in their ability to transform the poor-quality meats and other ingredients they were given for their own consumption into delicious meals.

A slave's daily diet was made up mostly of vegetables, such as wild greens and onions, and cornmeal. Instead of being used as main ingredients, "side" meats such as salt pork and animal fats were used to enhance the flavor of vegetables. Most of the "soul food" that is part of the African-American culinary heritage is a direct result of slave cooks "making do" with the few foodstuffs they received.

Plantation kitchens were the slave cooks' domain, and where they reigned supreme. An unhappy cook had many deadly ways of exacting vengeance on the slave owner, which may be why slave cooks won a little more consideration from the white household than did other slaves. The landscape architect Frederick Law Olmsted, in a book called *The Cotton Kingdom* about his travels through the South in the mid-1800s, noted that the mistresses of the plantations he visited seemed to know very little about cooking and were happy to leave their kitchens in the hands of their cooks. On some plantations, the cook was also responsible for planning the meals and procuring all the food.

When emancipation came, many slave cooks abandoned their pots and pans to find a new way of life. This left their former masters and mistresses in a quandary, and the popularity of cookbooks greatly increased at this time. The introduction to *The Picayune's Creole Cook Book*, published in New Orleans in 1885, laments "the passing of the faithful old negro cooks—the mammies," which "forced the ladies of the present day to...acquaint themselves thoroughly with the art of cooking...to assist them in this, to preserve to future generations the many excellent and matchless recipes of our New Orleans cuisine, to gather these up from the lips of the old Creole negro cooks and the grand old housekeepers who still survive, ere they, too, pass away, and Creole cookery, with all its delightful combinations and possibilities, will have become a lost art."

Slave cooks created recipes that made the South famous for its food. Although we do not know all the names of those who devised the dishes contained in this chapter, their delicious contribution to American cuisine has not been forgotten.

Condiments

Willie Mae's Green Tomato Chow-Chow

YIELD: ABOUT 8 CUPS

My grandmother Willie Mae Davis's chow-chow is legendary in my family. It's wonderful with a bowl of black-eyed peas or as a condiment with a mess of greens. Grandma Davis used pickling spice, a fragrant combination of ingredients including dill seeds, peppercorns, cinnamon sticks, ginger, allspice, juniper berries, mace, bay leaves, and cloves all prepackaged and available at most supermarkets. Grandma Davis canned her chow-chow, but it will keep in an airtight container in the refrigerator for about seven days.

2 cups washed, cored, and quartered green tomatoes
2 cups chopped green cabbage
1 large cucumber, peeled and chopped
1 cup chopped white onion

1 1/2 cups apple cider vinegar
1/2 cup sugar
1 tablespoon salt
1 tablespoon pickling spice

1. Place small quantities of each of the vegetables in a food processor and, working in batches, pulse 7 or 8 times until all the vegetables are finely chopped; do not overprocess. Place the vegetables in a large bowl and set aside.

2. In a large pot, bring the vinegar, sugar, salt, and pickling spice to a boil.

3. Add the vegetables to the vinegar mixture. Boil 8 to 10 minutes, stirring occasionally. Put the chow-chow in an airtight container and refrigerate immediately.

Salads

Fruit Salad

YIELD: 6 SERVINGS

In slavery times, fruit deserts were common. I love the contrasts of taste and color that a multi-hued fruit salad adds to a meal.

6 apples (Red Delicious, Golden Delicious,
 Gala, or Braeburn)
6 bananas, peeled
2 oranges, peeled
1 cup walnuts, coarsely chopped

DRESSING:
1 cup heavy cream
1 tablespoon all-purpose flour, mixed with
 a few drops of water to make a paste
3 tablespoons white vinegar
2 tablespoons butter
2 tablespoons sugar
1/8 teaspoon salt
1 egg white, beaten

1. Cut all the fruit into small cubes and put into a large bowl. Stir in the nuts.

2. To make the dressing: In a saucepan over low heat, simmer all the ingredients except the egg white, about 5 minutes, or until the mixture begins to boil. Remove from the heat immediately. Cool until the dressing is barely warm to the touch. Fold in the beaten egg white. Pour the dressing over the fruit, mixing gently to coat each piece. Refrigerate until chilled, about 1 hour.

Cabbage Slaw

YIELD: 8 TO 10 SERVINGS

1 (1 1/2-pound) head cabbage
1 onion
1/2 cup cider vinegar
1/2 cup sugar

2 1/2 tablespoons vegetable oil
1 1/2 tablespoons prepared mustard
1 1/2 teaspoons salt
1/2 teaspoon celery seed

1. Grate the cabbage and onion and place them in a large bowl. In a small saucepan, bring the remaining ingredients to a boil, stirring often. Cool the mixture and pour over the cabbage and onion and toss well. Cover and put in an airtight container. Refrigerate several hours before serving. The slaw will keep well for about a week.

Picnic Potato Salad

YIELD: 6 SERVINGS

There's no law that says you can only eat potato salad in the summertime. But I never think about eating it unless it's hot outside and the smell of hickory smoke from the grill hangs in the air.

5 medium red-skin potatoes
4 hard-cooked eggs, diced, plus 1 hard-
 cooked egg sliced in rounds (optional)
4 stalks celery, diced
3 pickles, chopped, with 1 tablespoon
 pickle juice
1/2 white onion, diced

1 teaspoon salt
1 teaspoon black pepper
1/2 teaspoon sugar
2 whole red pimientos, chopped
5 tablespoons mayonnaise
2 teaspoons prepared mustard
1/4 teaspoon paprika

1. Boil the potatoes until fork-tender, 15 to 20 minutes. Refrigerate until cool, then peel and dice.

2. Add the diced egg, celery, pickles and juice, onion, salt, black pepper, sugar, pimientos, mayonnaise, and mustard. Combine well. Taste and correct the seasonings. Decorate the salad with the sliced egg, if desired, and sprinkle the paprika over the top. Refrigerate.

Main Dishes

Beans and Neck Bones

YIELD: 4 SERVINGS

Fat hogs don't have much to brag on when killing time comes. —Slave proverb

1 cup dried pinto beans or lima beans,
    soaked overnight in water to cover
2 pounds fresh pork neck bones, cracked
    and washed
1 teaspoon salt

1 teaspoon black pepper
2 onions, chopped
1 teaspoon dried thyme
6 cups water

1. Drain the soaking water from the beans and discard any beans that are discolored. Combine the beans and the remaining ingredients in a large pot. Cover and bring to a boil. Reduce the heat and simmer 1 1/2 to 2 hours, stirring frequently and adding more water as needed. The water should just cover the meat and beans throughout the cooking time. Taste and correct the seasonings.

Baked Chicken with Cornbread Dressing

YIELD: 8 SERVINGS

1 teaspoon salt
1 teaspoon black pepper
2 teaspoons poultry seasoning
1 teaspoon garlic powder
1 (5- to 7-pound) roasting chicken
2 bay leaves
3 stalks celery, chopped
2 large onions, chopped

DRESSING:
4 cups crumbled cornbread
1 cup crumbled day-old bread or
    dinner rolls
1/2 cup sliced mushrooms
1/2 teaspoon dried sage
1/2 teaspoon dried thyme
4 tablespoons (1/2 stick) butter, melted
1 teaspoon salt
1 teaspoon black pepper
2 1/2 cups chicken broth
Parsley sprigs, for garnish

1. Combine the salt, black pepper, poultry seasoning, and garlic powder; rub the seasonings inside the chicken and all over the skin. Put the chicken in a large, heavy pot. Add the bay leaves, celery, and onions and enough water to cover. Bring the ingredients to a boil, then reduce the heat, cover, and simmer until the chicken is tender, about 1 hour.

2. Preheat the oven to 400 degrees. Remove the chicken from the broth and set it in a shallow roasting pan. Strain the broth through a sieve, reserving 2 1/2 cups of the broth, and reserving the vegetables to use in the dressing. Discard the bay leaves.

3. To prepare the dressing: Combine all the dressing ingredients except the broth and parsley in a baking pan. Add the celery and onions that were simmered with the chicken, then add the broth, 1/4 cup at a time, until the dressing is moist but not soupy, with a consistency of mush.

4. Bake the chicken and the dressing, uncovered, for 30 to 40 minutes, or until the chicken is golden brown and the dressing is firm but still moist.

5. Serve the chicken in the center of a platter surrounded by the dressing and garnished with parsley.

Chicken and Dumplings

YIELD: 4 TO 6 SERVINGS

Lazy folks' stomachs don't get tired. —Slave proverb

1 (3- to 4-pound) fryer chicken, cut into
    8 pieces
1 teaspoon salt
1 teaspoon black pepper
1/4 teaspoon sweet paprika
1/8 teaspoon ground nutmeg
All-purpose flour, for dredging
6 tablespoons bacon drippings or butter
1 medium onion, chopped
1 green bell pepper, seeded and diced
1 stalk celery, chopped
2 carrots, sliced

1 bay leaf
6 cups water
1 cup fresh, frozen, or canned whole-
    kernel corn

DUMPLINGS:
1 1/4 cups all-purpose flour
1 1/2 teaspoons baking powder
1 teaspoon salt
1 egg, beaten
1/2 cup milk
1 tablespoon butter, melted

1. Season the chicken with the salt, black pepper, paprika, and nutmeg, then dredge in flour. In a skillet over medium heat, heat 2 tablespoons of the bacon drippings or butter, add the onion and cook until golden. Remove the onion from the skillet and reserve.

2. Add the remaining 4 tablespoons drippings or butter to the skillet. Brown the chicken in batches on both sides. As they brown, place the chicken pieces in a large pot. Add the onion, green bell pepper, celery, carrots, bay leaf, and water. Bring to a boil. Reduce the heat, cover, and simmer 30 minutes.

3. While the chicken is simmering, prepare the dumplings: In a bowl sift together the flour, baking powder, and salt. Add the egg, milk, and melted butter. Blend the ingredients until a soft dough forms.

4. Remove the lid from the pot and add the corn to the chicken. Drop the dumpling batter by tablespoonfuls into the pot. Cover the pot and simmer 20 minutes. Do not remove the cover or stir. Remove the bay leaf before serving.

Chicken with Peaches

YIELD: 6 SERVINGS

The peaches and orange juice give this chicken a fresh new taste, a little sweet and slightly tangy. The finished dish looks pretty, too.

1 (3- to 4-pound) chicken, cut into 8 pieces
1 cup all-purpose flour
1 teaspoon dried sage
1 teaspoon dried thyme
2 teaspoons salt
1 teaspoon black pepper
1½ cups vegetable oil

2½ cups sliced canned peaches
1½ cups orange juice
3 tablespoons packed brown sugar
3 tablespoons white vinegar
1½ teaspoons ground nutmeg
1½ teaspoons dried basil
2 cloves garlic, chopped

1. Wash the chicken pieces and pat dry. On a plate, combine the flour, sage, thyme, salt, and black pepper. Dredge the chicken pieces in the seasoned flour. In a heavy skillet, heat the oil over high heat until hot but not smoking; brown the chicken well on all sides. Remove the chicken to a platter. Pour off the grease but reserve the pan drippings.

2. In a saucepan, combine the remaining ingredients. Cover tightly and simmer 10 minutes. Add one third of the fruit sauce to the pan drippings in the skillet and simmer over low heat, stirring. Return the chicken to the pan and cover with the remaining fruit sauce. Cover tightly. Simmer 20 minutes, or until the chicken is done.

Also pictured: Dinner Rolls (page 246)

Chicken Pie

YIELD: 8 SERVINGS

You can't tell much about chicken pie until you get through the crust. —Slave proverb

This is an old recipe but you can modernize it by using a commercially prepared rotisserie chicken and cooking the vegetables in chicken broth until the vegetables are tender instead of cooking the chicken as directed in the recipe. You'll save time without sacrificing any flavor!

1 (4- to 5-pound) chicken, cut into 8 pieces

1/2 cup minced onion

1/2 cup minced celery

2 bay leaves

1 teaspoon dried thyme

1 teaspoon dried sage

1 teaspoon salt

1 teaspoon black pepper

3 tablespoons butter

3 tablespoons all-purpose flour

1 cup milk

CRUST:

2 cups all-purpose flour

2 teaspoons baking powder

1 teaspoon salt

4 tablespoons (1/2 stick) cold butter

1 egg

2 cups milk

1. To prepare the chicken: Place the chicken in a pot with the onion, celery, bay leaves, thyme, sage, salt, and black pepper. Cover with water, bring to a boil and then turn the heat down to a simmer until the chicken is cooked through, about 45 minutes. Strain the broth, reserving 2 cups along with the vegetables. Discard the bay leaves. When cool enough to handle, remove the chicken from the bones and put the meat in a 12x15-inch baking dish or a deep casserole.

2. In a small saucepan, melt the 3 tablespoons butter, stir in the flour, and blend. Whisk the reserved 2 cups broth and the milk into the flour mixture and cook until it becomes a thin gravy, about 5 minutes. Add the reserved vegetables and pour the gravy over the chicken.

3. To prepare the crust: Preheat the oven to 350 degrees. Sift together the dry ingredients, then cut in the butter. In a small bowl, beat together the egg and milk and stir the mixture into the flour mixture until smooth. You will have a thin batter. Pour over the chicken and gravy and bake for 30 minutes, until the crust is golden brown and the juices are bubbling.

Chitlins

YIELD: 8 TO 10 SERVINGS

Chitlins, or chitterlings, the small intestines of the pig, are a traditional African-American dish. When it was hog-butchering time, the hams, pork chops, and roasts made their way to the master's dinner table. The chitlins went to the slaves. Ingenious African-American cooks prepared them in such a delicious way that the recipe has traveled down through history. My family considers chitlins a special treat on Thanksgiving, Christmas, and New Year's Day. Fix a pot of chitlins, add a side dish of greens and a bottle of hot sauce, and you're ready for a memorable meal.

2 cups white vinegar

2 cups salt

10 pounds chitlins

2 hog maws

2 cups coarsely chopped onion

2 fresh hot cayenne peppers, each about
   3 inches long, washed and stemmed

$1^{1}/_{2}$ cups coarsely chopped celery

1 teaspoon black pepper

1 green bell pepper, seeded and
   coarsely chopped

3 cups water

1. Fill a large basin with cold water and stir in the vinegar and salt. Drop in the chitlins and hog maws and let them soak for 30 minutes. Drain off the water and refill the basin with cold water. Peel off and discard most of the fat from the chitlins and hog maws. Turn the chitlins inside out and peel away the fat there also. Drain off the water and discard the fat. Rinse the meat under cold running water. Soak the chitlins and hog maws in fresh cold water 1 to 2 hours longer, changing the water several times. Rinse the meat again under cold running water and check the chitlins, inside and out, to make sure they are free of dirt.

2. Place the chitlins in a large pot with a tight-fitting lid. Add the onion, cayenne peppers, celery, black pepper, green bell pepper, and 3 cups water and bring to a boil over high heat. Cover the pot, reduce the heat to low, and simmer about 3 hours, or until almost all the liquid has evaporated and the chitlins and hog maws are tender. Remove the cayenne peppers.

Southern Fried Chicken

YIELD: 4 TO 6 SERVINGS

Southern fried chicken has been a favorite dish for more than 150 years. There are as many variations on this recipe as there are people who like the dish, but the chicken should always be brown and crisp outside and moist and tender inside. I learned the trick of perfecting fried chicken from my friend, Elizabeth Ray. She's the mother of twelve children, and grew up on a farm, so she's fried a lot of chicken in her time. Covering the frying pan with a tight-fitting lid half-way through the cooking process is her tip for fried chicken that will be beautifully crisp on the outside and perfectly cooked on the inside.

1 (2- to 3-pound) fryer chicken, cut into
    8 pieces
Buttermilk, to cover chicken
3 to 4 tablespoons Tabasco sauce
1 1/2 cups all-purpose flour
1 teaspoon salt

1 teaspoon black pepper
1 teaspoon hot or sweet paprika
1 teaspoon garlic powder
1 teaspoon poultry seasoning
2 cups vegetable oil
2 tablespoons butter

1. Put the chicken pieces in a large mixing bowl and add enough buttermilk to cover. Add the Tabasco and refrigerate 1 hour.

2. Combine the flour, salt, pepper, paprika, garlic powder, and poultry seasoning in a large, resealable plastic bag. Shake to blend. Remove the chicken pieces from the buttermilk, shaking off the excess liquid. Drop the chicken pieces, 1 at a time, into the seasoned flour and shake until well coated. Place the coated pieces on a plate and set aside in the refrigerator for 30 minutes.

3. In a large heavy skillet (preferably cast iron) over high heat, heat the oil and butter until a pinch of flour sizzles when sprinkled on top. Reduce the heat to medium and cook the first batch of chicken pieces, dark meat first and then the white pieces, without the pieces touching (don't crowd them!). Cover the pan with a tight-fitting lid. Cook until the pieces are golden brown on one side, 10 to 15 minutes. Remove the cover and turn the pieces over. Continue cooking, uncovered, 10 to 12 minutes, or until the chicken pieces are cooked through completely. Drain on paper towels. If you're cooking the chicken in batches, keep the pieces warm in a 200-degree oven until all the pieces have finished frying.

Tripe

YIELD: 4 SERVINGS

Slaves often were given tripe, a section of a cow's stomach, as well as other poor cuts of meat. Once again, the slaves learned to make do and create a tasty meal.

1 pound honeycomb tripe

1 tablespoon salt

1 onion, chopped

1/4 teaspoon black pepper

1. Wash the tripe and cover it with water in a pot. Add the salt, onion, and black pepper. Bring the ingredients to a boil, then lower the heat. Cover and simmer for 1 hour, or until the meat is fork-tender.

Fried Fish

YIELD: 2 OR 3 SMALL FISH PER SERVING

2 or 3 small fish (mackerel, whiting, porgies, or butterfish) per person (about 1/2 pound each)

1 cup all-purpose flour

1 cup cornmeal

1 teaspoon salt

1 teaspoon black pepper

1 teaspoon poultry seasoning

1 1/2 cups shortening or vegetable oil

1. Wash and clean the fish, making sure the fins and all scales are removed. In a flat dish, combine the flour, cornmeal, salt, pepper, and poultry seasoning and dredge the fish in the flour mixture until well coated. Place on a plate and set in refrigerator for 30 minutes.

2. In a skillet, heat the shortening over high heat until it is very hot but not smoking. Fry the fish until browned on both sides, about 3 minutes per side. Drain on paper towels.

Hoppin' John

YIELD: 10 SERVINGS

Black-eyed peas were transported from Africa to the West Indies and then into the Carolinas before the 1700s. Hoppin' John is an African dish that has been adapted for American tastes and is commonly served on New Year's Day.

Some say the dish got its name from the word bahatta-kachang, meaning peas with cooked rice, which is of East African origin. Others say the name comes from the tradition of having the children of the family hop around the table on New Year's Day before eating the dish. All I know is that you're a fortunate person if you can sit down to a dish of Hoppin' John.

1 pound dried black-eyed peas, picked over
   and soaked overnight in 6 cups water
1/2 pound smoked ham hocks
1 onion, sliced

1 whole jalapeño or cayenne pepper
1 teaspoon salt
1 cup cooked rice

1. Place the peas and water in a pot over moderate heat and add the ham hocks, onion, hot pepper, and salt. Bring to a boil, reduce the heat to low, cover, and simmer 1 to 1 1/2 hours, or until the peas and meat are tender. Remove the hot pepper.

2. Remove skin and bones from the hocks and cut the meat into small pieces. Return the meat to the pot. Add the cooked rice to the pot and heat about 5 minutes.

Liver and Onions

YIELD: 6 SERVINGS

> The fat cow ain't got much confidence in a butcher. —Slave proverb

2 pounds calf's liver, thinly sliced

2 cups milk

3/4 cup vegetable oil

1 onion, sliced

2 teaspoons salt

2 teaspoons black pepper

2 teaspoons garlic powder

2 teaspoons onion powder

1 cup all-purpose flour

1/2 cup warm water

1 tablespoon steak sauce

1. Soak the liver in the milk for 2 hours or overnight. Drain the milk and pat the liver with a paper towel until dry. In a skillet over medium heat, heat 1/4 cup oil until hot but not smoking; sauté the onion until tender and golden. Remove the onion from the skillet and set aside.

2. Sprinkle 1 teaspoon salt, 1 teaspoon black pepper, 1 teaspoon garlic powder, and 1 teaspoon onion powder on the liver. Place the flour in a bowl and add the remaining salt, pepper, garlic powder, and onion powder to the flour and mix well. Set aside 4 tablespoons of the seasoned flour for the gravy.

3. Dredge the liver in the remaining seasoned flour until well coated. Place the pan over medium heat, add 1/4 cup oil to the pan. Gently brown the liver on both sides, 5 to 7 minutes. Remove the liver from the pan and set it aside.

4. Add the remaining 1/4 cup oil to the pan to heat over medium heat. Add the reserved 4 tablespoons seasoned flour to the pan. Let the flour cook for a few minutes, stirring occasionally to brown the flour and remove the powdery taste.

5. Stirring constantly to prevent the flour from clumping, slowly add the warm water to the skillet. Bring the mixture to a boil and continue to stir to keep the gravy smooth while it thickens. If the gravy is too thick, add more warm water, a few tablespoons at a time. Stir in the steak sauce and add in the cooked onion. Place the liver back into the pan to reheat and coat each piece with the gravy. Cover, and simmer until the liver is fork-tender, about 10 minutes. Serve immediately.

Baked Macaroni and Cheese

YIELD: 8 SERVINGS

James Hemings was President Thomas Jefferson's slave chef. While Jefferson was given credit for his gardens and dinner parties, it was slave labor that planted and tended the crops and created the dishes that were served to Jefferson's guests. Hemings was trained in France and created dishes that introduced an exciting new cuisine to America. "Thomas Jefferson came home from France so Frenchified that he abjured his native victuals," said Jefferson's political rival Patrick Henry. In fact, it was Hemings who creatively combined the elements of French cuisine with American cooking. For Jefferson and his guests he prepared cornbread stuffing, waffles, and ice cream, unusual dishes at that time. Hemings also introduced the use of almonds, raisins, and vanilla. You could say that Hemings cooked his way to freedom. In 1793, Jefferson signed a document that emancipated Hemings if he promised to train a new chef for Monticello. Hemings was among the first cooks in America to serve macaroni.

This version of macaroni and cheese is also an old one.

6 cups water

1 tablespoon salt

2 cups elbow macaroni

6 tablespoons butter, softened, plus more for dish

2 large eggs

2 cups evaporated milk

1 teaspoon salt

2 dashes Tabasco sauce

1 pound extra-sharp cheddar cheese, grated

1/2 cup grated American cheese

1/2 teaspoon sweet paprika

1. Preheat the oven to 350 degrees. Put the water and salt in a heavy saucepan and bring to a boil. Slowly stir in the macaroni. Boil 12 minutes, stirring occasionally. The macaroni should be firm but tender. Pour the macaroni into a colander and rinse with a little cold water. Drain. Toss the macaroni with the butter and set aside.

2. In a small bowl, beat the eggs until light yellow. Add the milk, salt, and Tabasco sauce. Butter a large casserole dish. Combine the cheddar and American cheeses.

3. In the casserole, alternate 1/2 cup layers of the cooked macaroni with layers of the mixed cheeses, ending with the cheeses on top. Pour the egg mixture slowly and evenly over the macaroni and cheese. Sprinkle with the paprika. Bake 30 to 40 minutes, until the custard is set and the top is bubbly and golden brown.

Also pictured: Old-Fashioned String Beans (page 146)

Ham Steak and Red-Eye Gravy

YIELD: 4 BREAKFAST SERVINGS

1 center slice country ham, about 3/8 inch
   thick
1 tablespoon butter
1 cup hot water

2 tablespoons brewed black coffee
1 teaspoon Tabasco
1 teaspoon black pepper

1. Soak the ham in cold water, 30 minutes to 1 hour, to remove the salt. Drain and pat dry.

2. In a heavy skillet, melt the butter over high heat until hot and the foam subsides. Turn the heat to medium and cook the ham 2 to 3 minutes per side, turning occasionally, until tender and brown. Remove the ham from the skillet and set aside in a warm place.

3. Turn the heat to high and add the hot water and the coffee to the skillet and cook, stirring to loosen all the browned particles and bits of meat. Boil 2 minutes. Season with hot sauce and black pepper. Pour the gravy over the ham. Slice ham into serving pieces and serve with eggs or over grits or biscuits, if desired.

Baked Rabbit

YIELD: 4 SERVINGS

My grandmother and great-grandmother often served the wild rabbit the men in the family shot in the winter months. They believed breeding rabbits shouldn't be eaten. Now you can find commercially raised rabbits year-round in most grocery stores. Rabbit tastes much like the dark meat of chicken. Because rabbits were once plentiful, it was not unusual to find a recipe for stewed, fried, or baked rabbit in the old Southern "receipt" books.

1 (3- to 4-pound) rabbit, skinned
1 1/2 tablespoons white vinegar
2 teaspoons salt
3 tablespoons butter
1/2 teaspoon black pepper
2 medium onions, chopped

1 carrot, diced
2 bay leaves
1 clove garlic, minced
2 stalks celery, diced
1 tablespoon all-purpose flour
3 tablespoons water

1. Preheat the oven to 350 degrees. Wash the rabbit and cut into serving pieces. Place the rabbit in a bowl and cover it with water. Add the vinegar and 1 teaspoon of the salt. Refrigerate 1 hour.

2. Drain off the liquid. In a medium skillet over medium-high heat, heat the butter. Season the rabbit pieces with the remaining teaspoon salt and the black pepper. Brown the rabbit pieces on both sides.

3. Put the rabbit in a casserole or roasting pan. Add the onions, carrot, bay leaves, garlic, and celery. Make a paste with the flour and 3 tablespoons water. Stir it into the liquid surrounding the rabbit to thicken it. Cover the casserole tightly, and bake until the meat is fork-tender, about 1 1/2 hours.

Vegetables

Cabbage and Cracklings

YIELD: 6 SERVINGS

Often all the slaves had for meat rations was pork skin. The slaves cooked the skin in a skillet until it crackled; hence the name for the delicious bits of skin and crisp meat that remained after the fat had been rendered from the pork skin. Slave cooks mixed the cracklings into their cornbread batter or cooked them with vegetables. Many grocery stores sell pork cracklings, or you can make your own at home. In a heavy skillet over moderate heat, cook 1 cup chopped salt pork or slab bacon for 10 minutes, until it is crisp and brown. Drain the fat and reserve it for frying. The crisp bits that are left are the cracklings.

1 (3-pound) head green cabbage, washed
1 onion, sliced
2 teaspoons bacon fat or butter
1/2 cup cracklings
1 teaspoon salt

1/4 teaspoon black pepper
1 teaspoon dried thyme
1/2 teaspoon sugar
1 cup water
1 teaspoon white vinegar

1. Core and coarsely chop the cabbage, discarding any yellow leaves. In a large pot over medium heat, brown the onion in the bacon fat or butter until golden. Add the cabbage, cracklings, salt, pepper, thyme, sugar, and water. Cover and cook over low heat 20 minutes, stirring often. Mix in the vinegar and cook the cabbage another 3 minutes.

Creamed Corn

YIELD: 6 SERVINGS

For years, my only acquaintance with creamed corn was with the canned variety. I didn't taste fresh creamed corn until I became an adult. An older friend showed me how to prepare the dish. The milk contained in the kernels of fresh corn gives this dish a wonderful taste. Try it; you'll never want canned "cream-style" corn again.

5 ears fresh corn (white is best)
1/2 to 1 cup milk, as needed
8 tablespoons (1 stick) butter
1 teaspoon salt

1/2 teaspoon sugar
1/8 teaspoon white pepper
1 teaspoon cornstarch, as needed
1 teaspoon cold milk, as needed

1. Shuck the corn and remove the silks carefully. You may want to use a soft brush so as not to break open the kernels. Rinse thoroughly. Pointing the end of the cob down into a bowl, use a sharp knife to gently remove the kernels. Do not try to remove the corn down to the cob all at once. Slice off one third of the kernel all around the cob, then another third. Cut the last third off close to the cob, then scrape the remaining corn milk into the bowl.

2. Put the corn and corn milk into a heavy skillet. Rinse out the bowl with a little water to get all the corn milk. If the corn is dry, add 1/2 cup milk to the skillet. If the corn is still dry, add a little more milk, up to another 1/2 cup.

3. Add the butter, salt, sugar, and white pepper to the skillet. Cover and simmer slowly, 10 minutes, stirring often.

4. The corn will become tender, and the sauce should thicken to the consistency of cream. If it is still watery, mix 1 teaspoon each of cornstarch and cold milk in a bowl. Add the cornstarch mixture to the corn while stirring. Simmer another 5 minutes, stirring often.

Fried Corn

YIELD: 6 SERVINGS

Fried corn has become my oldest sister, Sandra's, specialty. Some recipes call for bacon fat instead of butter, but I think her version gives the corn a better flavor.

8 tablespoons (1 stick) butter
4 cups fresh corn kernels, or 2 (16-ounce) packages frozen corn

1/2 cup sugar
1/2 teaspoon salt

1. In a medium skillet, melt 1 stick of butter. Add the corn, sugar, and salt and stir well. Cook over low heat for 15 minutes, stirring frequently.

Corn Pudding

YIELD: 4 SERVINGS

Heap of good cotton stalks get chopped up from associating with weeds.
—Slave proverb

2 eggs
4 tablespoons (1/2 stick) butter, melted and cooled, plus more for dish
1 cup milk
3 tablespoons sugar

2 cups canned or frozen corn kernels
2 tablespoons all-purpose flour
1 teaspoon salt
1/2 teaspoon black pepper
1/2 teaspoon ground nutmeg

1. Preheat the oven to 350 degrees. In a large mixing bowl, beat the eggs. Stir in the melted butter. Add the milk and sugar, combining well. Add the remaining ingredients and combine well.

2. Grease a 1-quart baking dish and pour the pudding into it. Bake 45 minutes, or until the custard is set and a knife inserted in the center comes out clean.

Fried Green Tomatoes

YIELD: 4 SERVINGS

Some food historians believe that recipes using tomatoes were introduced to the Americas by slave cooks. Fried green tomatoes are traditionally served with bacon and eggs at breakfast time in the South.

3 firm green tomatoes, stemmed and
   sliced 1/2 inch thick

2 teaspoons salt

2 teaspoons black pepper

2 teaspoons garlic powder

4 tablespoons (1/2 stick) butter

1/4 cup olive oil

1/2 cup all-purpose flour

2 eggs, beaten

1/2 cup cornmeal

1/4 teaspoon cayenne pepper

1. Season the tomatoes with 1 teaspoon of the salt, 1 teaspoon black pepper, and 1 teaspoon garlic powder. Set aside for 15 minutes.

2. In a skillet over medium heat, melt the butter and add the oil. Place the flour, the eggs, and the cornmeal in separate shallow dishes and season each dish with the cayenne pepper and the remaining salt, black pepper, and garlic powder.

3. Dredge the tomato slices in the flour, dip them into the eggs, and then dredge them in the cornmeal. Sauté the battered slices in the oil, cooking 3 to 5 minutes on 1 side; then flip and cook until golden brown on both sides.

Green Beans with Okra

YIELD: 6 SERVINGS

I had never heard of preparing green beans with okra until the host of a talk show told me about her family's recipe. All I can say is, don't knock it until you've tried it!

4 slices lean bacon, cut into 1/2-inch dice
1/2 cup chopped scallions
1 box (10 ounces) frozen green beans, or
    1 pound fresh green beans, washed,
    snapped, and with strings removed

1/2 cup water
8 to 12 baby okra
1 teaspoon salt
1/4 teaspoon black pepper
11/2 teaspoons red wine vinegar

1. In a large skillet, fry the bacon until brown and crisp. Place bacon on a paper towel to drain.

2. Sauté the scallions in the bacon fat 2 to 3 minutes, until they are soft but not brown. Add the green beans to the skillet, stirring them until they are well coated with the bacon fat. Add the water and the okra. Cover the pan tightly. Cook over low heat for 15 to 20 minutes, or until the vegetables are tender. Sprinkle with the salt and black pepper, stir in the vinegar, and remove from the heat. Place the green beans and okra in a serving dish and sprinkle with the bacon.

New Potatoes and Snap Beans

YIELD: 6 SERVINGS

The dinner bell is always in tune. —Slave proverb

2 pounds fresh beans (snap beans, green
    beans, or string beans)
1 small ham hock
1 onion, sliced

11/2 teaspoons salt
11/2 teaspoons black pepper
11/2 teaspoons dried thyme
1 pound small new potatoes

1. Snap the ends off the beans, string them, and break them into pieces 2 or 3 inches long. Put the ham hock in a large pot with water to cover. Turn the heat to moderate and cook the ham hock, covered, about 20 minutes. Add the beans and onion, 1/2 teaspoon each of the salt, black pepper, and thyme.

2. Wash the potatoes thoroughly. Peel away a band of skin around the middle of each potato. Place the potatoes on top of the beans, sprinkling them well with the remaining 1 teaspoon each salt, pepper, and thyme. Cover the pot and continue cooking until the potatoes and beans are tender when tested with a fork, 15 to 20 minutes. Add more water if needed.

Greens and Okra

YIELD: 6 TO 8 SERVINGS

Waiting on the table is a powerful way to work up an appetite. —Slave proverb

2 cups chopped ham
3 cups water
4 bunches collard greens
1/2 tablespoon salt

1/2 teaspoon sugar
1 or 2 jalapeño peppers or dried cayenne
  pepper pods, to taste
8 to 12 small okra, stemmed

1. In a heavy pot or Dutch oven, simmer the ham in the water until it is tender and the fat dissolves, 15 to 20 minutes.

2. Cut the tough stems and yellow leaves from the greens and discard. Gently rub the leaves with your fingers under warm running water. Cut the greens into large pieces. Let the leaves soak in warm, salted water for 10 minutes. Rinse with cool water and drain in a colander.

3. Add the salt, sugar, and peppers to the ham, then add the greens. Stir every 15 minutes until the greens are wilted but not quite tender, 30 to 45 minutes.

4. Layer the okra on top of the greens. Cover and continue cooking the greens and okra 20 minutes, or until tender, stirring occasionally and adding hot water as needed to prevent the greens from sticking. Remove peppers and serve hot.

Okra Gumbo

The preparation of okra is a gift to America from African cooks who were enslaved here. Both the word gumbo, which means "okra" in some African languages, and the recipe of the same name are African imports. There are as many variations of this recipe as there are cooks, from difficult roux-based gumbos to simpler okra-based ones. All are delicious served with a bowl of hot, fluffy rice.

12 tablespoons (1½ sticks) butter

3 cups chopped onion

1 clove garlic, minced

8 cups sliced okra

7 cups chopped tomatoes

2 tablespoons dried parsley

1 teaspoon sweet paprika

1 teaspoon salt

1 teaspoon black pepper

Juice of ½ lemon

1 tablespoon sugar

1 teaspoon Worcestershire sauce

3 tablespoons ketchup

1. In a large skillet over medium heat, melt 4 tablespoons of the butter. Sauté the onion and garlic until golden, about 5 minutes. Remove the onion and garlic with a slotted spoon and set aside. Melt the remaining 8 tablespoons butter in the skillet, add the okra, and simmer 10 minutes, stirring often. Add the remaining ingredients and reserved onion and garlic, cover, and simmer, stirring occasionally, 30 to 40 minutes.

Mustard and Turnip Greens

YIELD: 8 TO 10 SERVINGS

Greens flavored with a "side meat" such as ham hocks or fatback were often served by slave cooks to their families as a main dish. When no side meat was available, bacon fat or a ham bone was used. Sometimes greens and vegetables with different flavors were mixed. Pot likker, the highly seasoned liquid that is left after the greens cook down, is full of vitamins and minerals. If greens were served one day, the leftover pot likker and a pan of cornbread often made the meal for the next. And the old song, "Ham bone, ham bone, where you been? Around the world and back again," refers to the slaves' practice of sharing a ham bone to flavor a pot of greens or beans, around the slave quarters and back to the owner of the ham bone.

2 ham hocks

3 pounds mustard greens

4 pounds turnip greens

2 teaspoons sugar

1 teaspoon Tabasco sauce

1. Place the ham hocks in a large pot. Cover with water. Bring to a boil, then reduce the heat and simmer, covered, 2 hours.

2. Cut the tough stems and yellow leaves from the greens and discard. Gently rub the leaves with your fingers under warm running water until clean. Cut the greens into large pieces. Let the leaves soak in warm, salted water 10 minutes. Rinse with cool water and drain in a colander.

3. Skim any fat from the liquid in which the ham hocks were cooked. Remove the hocks and cut the meat into bite-size pieces, discarding the skin and bones. Return the meat to the pot and add the sugar and Tabasco sauce. Add as many greens as will fit in the pot. Cover and cook down until the greens are wilted, then add more greens until all the greens are in the pot. Continue cooking, covered, until the greens are tender, about 1 1/2 hours. Add more hot water, if necessary.

Glazed Yellow Turnips

YIELD: 6 SERVINGS

Yellow turnips have a sweeter flavor if selected after the first fall frost.

2¹/₂ cups peeled diced turnips
3 tablespoons butter
3 tablespoons light corn syrup

¹/₄ teaspoon ground nutmeg
1 teaspoon salt
1 teaspoon black pepper, or to taste

1. Put the turnips in a saucepan and cover with water. Boil until tender, 15 to 20 minutes. Drain.

2. In a skillet over medium heat, melt the butter. Add the turnips, corn syrup, nutmeg, salt, and black pepper. Cook, stirring frequently, about 10 minutes, or until the turnips are lightly browned.

Honey-Baked Onions

YIELD: 8 SERVINGS

Ain't much difference between a yellowjacket and a hornet when they both get under your clothes. —Slave proverb

4 large sweet white onions
2 tablespoons butter, melted, plus more
   for dish

1¹/₂ cups tomato juice
1¹/₂ cups water
2 tablespoons honey

1. Preheat the oven to 325 degrees. Peel the onions and discard the skins, then cut in half. Butter a baking dish and arrange the onions cut side up in the dish. In a bowl, combine 2 tablespoons melted butter and the rest of the ingredients. Pour the sauce over the onions, brushing them to coat. Bake 1 hour, or until the onions are soft.

Old-Fashioned String Beans

YIELD: 4 SERVINGS

Don't say more with your mouth than your back can stand. —Slave proverb

4 slices lean bacon, diced
1/2 cup thinly sliced scallions
1 pound green beans, washed, snapped,
   and strings removed
1 tablespoon cold water

1 teaspoon salt
1 teaspoon black pepper
1 1/2 teaspoons red wine vinegar
2 tablespoons finely cut fresh mint leaves

1. In a large skillet over medium heat, fry the bacon, turning the pieces frequently until brown and crisp. Remove the bacon pieces with a slotted spoon and drain on a paper towel.

2. Cook the scallions in the bacon fat over moderate heat 3 to 4 minutes, until they are soft but not brown. Add the beans to the skillet, stirring them until they are well coated with the bacon fat. Add 1 tablespoon cold water and cover the pan tightly. Cook over low heat 5 minutes, then uncover the pan and continue to cook until the beans are crisp-tender. Sprinkle the beans with the salt and black pepper, stir in the vinegar, and remove from the heat. Put the beans in a serving dish, crumble the bacon, and sprinkle the beans with the bacon pieces and mint.

Candied Yams

YIELD: 4 SERVINGS

Eating yams makes you smile all over. —Slave proverb

2 tablespoons butter, plus more for dish
2 large yams or sweet potatoes, peeled
   and sliced 1/2 inch thick
1 teaspoon ground cinnamon

1/2 cup sugar
1/2 teaspoon ground nutmeg
2/3 cup evaporated milk
1/3 cup water

1. Preheat the oven to 350 degrees; grease a square baking dish with butter. Layer half the yams or sweet potatoes in the dish. In a small bowl, combine the cinnamon, sugar, and nutmeg. Sprinkle half the mixture over the yams. Dot the yams with half the butter. Layer on the rest of the yams, sprinkle with the remaining sugar mixture, and dot with the remaining butter. Mix the milk and water and pour over the yams. Cover and bake, 45 minutes.

2. Increase the oven temperature to 400 degrees. Uncover the casserole and bake another 10 minutes, until the yams are golden brown and tender.

Southern Succotash

YIELD: 4 SERVINGS

Corn mixed with beans became a staple in the South as the Civil War dragged on through the 1860s and in its aftermath, as times became harder and harder. Newly freed blacks may have fared a little better than newly poor whites because they already knew how to make do with the food that was available. Succotash, originally a Native American recipe, became a popular main dish. Succotash is especially delicious with buttered cornbread.

1 cup dried baby lima beans
3 cups water
1 teaspoon salt
1 (28-ounce) can whole tomatoes with liquid
1/4 teaspoon dried thyme

2 small bay leaves
2 tablespoons chopped green bell pepper
1 tablespoon bacon fat or butter
1 cup fresh, frozen, or canned corn kernels
1 tablespoon sugar

1. Put all the ingredients except the corn and sugar in a large pot over high heat. Bring to a boil. Cover and turn the heat down to low. Simmer 1 1/2 hours, adding more water as needed to cover the beans and vegetables.

2. Stir in the corn and sugar. Cover and cook another 25 minutes, stirring occasionally.

Rice

Jefferson Rice
(Pilau with Pine Nuts and Pistachios)

YIELD: 4 TO 6 SERVINGS

President Thomas Jefferson lived a life of great comfort at Monticello, his plantation in Virginia. His well-being was ensured by numerous slaves, including the chef James Hemings and his sister Sally. Whether Jefferson fathered Sally Hemings's son, Thomas Woodson, and her five other children, two of whom died in infancy, has long been a matter of hot debate among historians. James and Sally Hemings traveled to France with Jefferson in 1785 when he was appointed minister to France. When Jefferson returned in 1789, James had received extensive training in French cuisine and Sally was pregnant with Thomas. This rice dish graced Jefferson's dinner table.

1 cup uncooked rice	1 teaspoon salt
1 cup homemade or canned chicken stock	1/2 cup pine nuts
1 cup water	1/4 cup shelled unsalted pistachios
4 tablespoons (1/2 stick) butter	1/4 teaspoon ground mace

1. In a colander, rinse the rice under cold running water. Drain. In a heavy saucepan over high heat, bring the chicken stock, 1 cup water, 1 tablespoon of the butter, and 1/2 teaspoon of the salt to a boil. Stir in the rice, cover tightly, and simmer over very low heat about 15 minutes, or until the rice is tender and the grains have absorbed all the liquid.

2. In a heavy skillet over moderate heat, melt the remaining 3 tablespoons butter. Stir in the pine nuts and pistachios and sauté until they are a delicate golden color. Remove the skillet from the heat. Put the cooked rice in a serving bowl and fluff it with a fork. Sprinkle the nuts over the rice and toss gently. Sprinkle the pilau with the mace and the remaining 1/2 teaspoon salt.

Red Rice

YIELD: 6 SERVINGS

> Promising talk don't cook rice. —Gullah proverb
>
> Many West Africans were enslaved on the Sea Islands off the coasts of Georgia and South Carolina, most planting and harvesting rice. Linguists have documented more than thirty different tribes and languages on the Sea Islands. To communicate with each other and with the white overseers, the captives devised a combination of African dialects and English that was called Gullah. Because Gullah was not a written language, much of it has been lost. However, remnants of the language and of the Sea Island culture, which is strongly rooted in African traditions, still survive among the descendants of the African captives.

6 slices lean bacon

1 cup finely chopped onion

1/2 red bell pepper, seeded and finely chopped

1 cup uncooked rice

1/8 teaspoon Tabasco sauce

1 teaspoon sweet paprika

1 teaspoon sugar

1 teaspoon salt

1 cup drained chopped canned tomatoes

11/2 cups cold water

1. In a heavy skillet, fry the bacon over medium-low heat until crisp and brown. Drain on paper towels, then crumble and set aside.

2. Pour off all but about 4 tablespoons of the fat remaining in the skillet and add the onion and red bell pepper. Cook over medium heat, stirring frequently, about 5 minutes. The onion should be soft but not brown. Add the rice and stir to coat the grains with the fat. Stir in the Tabasco sauce, paprika, sugar, salt, tomatoes, and 11/2 cups water. Bring the mixture to a boil over high heat, cover tightly, and reduce the heat to very low. Simmer about 15 minutes, or until all the liquid has evaporated and the rice is tender.

3. Remove the skillet from the heat and set aside, covered, for 10 minutes. Serve the rice in a bowl with the crumbled bacon on top.

Eggs

Eggs and Green Onions

YIELD: 6 SERVINGS

A friend told me he always felt special when his mother fixed eggs and green onions for breakfast—that is, until his cousins came for a visit. They informed him that eggs and green onions was poor folks' food. My friend said he never realized how poor he was until they told him. I think this is a special breakfast, fit for a king; and now so does he.

2 tablespoons butter

12 scallions (green onions), including
   tops, chopped fine

6 eggs

1/4 cup light cream

1/2 teaspoon salt

1/8 teaspoon black pepper

1 cup cold cooked rice

1. In a skillet over low heat, melt the butter. Add the scallions and cook until soft, 3 or 4 minutes. Beat the eggs and blend in the cream, salt, and black pepper. Pour the egg mixture into the skillet and cook, stirring constantly, until the eggs are almost done. Stir in the rice and cook until heated through, about 5 minutes.

Breakfast Casserole

YIELD: 6 SERVINGS

Rich and poor, black and white,
Lutheran and Campbellite,
Jews and Southern Jesuits,
All acknowledge buttered grits.
—Roy Blount, Jr., One Fell Soup

1 cup white hominy grits, or white hominy
    5-minute quick grits
2 slices bacon, fried until crisp, and
    crumbled

4 tablespoons (1/2 stick) butter
6 eggs
1 teaspoon salt
1 teaspoon black pepper

1. Preheat the oven to 350 degrees. Prepare the grits according to the package directions. Stir in the bacon bits and 2 tablespoons of the butter.

2. Pour the grits mixture into an ungreased 7x11-inch baking dish. With the back of a spoon, make 6 depressions in the grits, about 2 inches apart. Carefully break 1 egg into each depression. Melt the remaining 2 tablespoons butter and pour over the eggs. Sprinkle with the salt and black pepper. Bake, uncovered, 15 minutes, or until the eggs are done.

Breads

Southern Pecan Biscuits

YIELD: ABOUT 2 DOZEN BISCUITS

Serve these biscuits with butter and pancake syrup and you'll be talking with a Southern drawl for the rest of the day. If you have leftover candied sweet potatoes or yams, they'll work fine. Just reduce the brown sugar by 1 tablespoon.

2 cups sifted all-purpose flour, plus more
 for dusting
4 teaspoons baking powder
1 cup cold mashed sweet potatoes
8 tablespoons (1 stick) butter or
 margarine, melted

2 tablespoons packed light brown sugar
2/3 cup milk, at room temperature
1/2 cup chopped pecans

1. Preheat the oven to 400 degrees. In a bowl, combine the flour and baking powder. In another large bowl, combine the sweet potatoes, butter, and brown sugar. Stir in the milk and the flour mixture alternately until the dough is smooth. Add the pecans.

2. Briefly knead the dough on a floured surface—just 3 or 4 times. Roll out to 1/2 inch thick. With a floured biscuit cutter, cut into 11/2-inch rounds. Place the biscuits on a lightly greased baking sheet, about 1 inch apart, and bake 15 minutes.

Beaten Biscuits

YIELD: ABOUT 40 BISCUITS

"In Virginia of the olden time, no breakfast or tea table was thought to be properly furnished without a plate of these indispensable biscuits.... Let one spend the night at some gentleman-farmer's home and the first sound heard in the morning, after the crowing of the cock, was the heavy, regular fall of the cook's axe, as she beat and beat her biscuit dough." —Mary Stuart Smith, Virginia Cookery Book, 1885

Many a slave cook started her day laboriously beating biscuit dough with the side of an ax or a heavy wooden mallet. Most recipes directed that the dough should be beaten "300 times for family, 500 for company." So when Miss Smith came to call on that gentleman farmer, the cook's work was almost doubled.

The food processor has eliminated the need to beat the dough with the side of an ax for hours at a time. Beating these biscuits does not make them light or fluffy. They are flaky and crisp, perfect as appetizers when split and sandwiched around thin slices of ham. They look a little different from the original version, but the taste should be about the same.

2 cups all-purpose flour

1/4 teaspoon salt

1/4 teaspoon baking soda

1 tablespoon sugar

1/4 cup vegetable shortening, plus more for pan

1/3 cup milk

1. Preheat the oven to 325 degrees. In a large bowl, sift together the flour, salt, baking soda, and sugar. Cut in the shortening with a pastry cutter or 2 knives, until the mixture resembles coarse meal. Slowly stir in the milk. The dough should be very stiff. Knead it just until smooth, then form it into a ball.

2. Put the dough blade in the food processor. Divide the dough into 6 balls and put all of them into the bowl of the food processor. Process for 2 minutes. Remove the dough from the bowl and knead lightly, rolling and folding a few times. Roll out the dough 1/4 inch thick. Using a biscuit cutter or the rim of a glass, cut into 1 1/2-inch rounds.

3. Grease a baking sheet and bake the biscuits 30 minutes, or until they are brown on the bottom and tan on top. They should be crisp, flaky, and light. The biscuits can be stored in the freezer, tightly wrapped, for up to 2 months.

Cornbread

YIELD: 6 SERVINGS

Cornbread has had many translations from Africa to America. It has become the bread of choice for Southerners. This is my favorite cornbread recipe. I triple it during the holidays and use it as the delicious base for my cornbread dressing. I always cook it in a cast iron skillet that my mother gave me. The skillet was originally owned by my grandmother, and it probably came from her mother. It hangs on display with my other cast iron pans. I always think about the women in my family whenever I use it, especially when I'm making cornbread.

1/3 cup vegetable shortening

1/2 cup yellow cornmeal

1/2 cup all-purpose flour

3 teaspoons baking powder

1 egg, beaten

1/3 cup water

1/2 teaspoon salt

1/3 cup sugar

2/3 cup evaporated milk

1. Preheat the oven to 400 degrees. In a cast iron skillet or 8-inch baking pan over moderate heat, melt the shortening. In a large mixing bowl, combine the remaining ingredients. Mix half the melted shortening into the batter, leaving the remaining half in the skillet. While the shortening in the skillet or pan is still hot, pour in the batter.

2. Bake the cornbread 15 minutes, or until the top is brown and the sides crisp.

Crackling Cornbread

YIELD: 4 TO 6 SERVINGS

Cracklings are the fried pieces of meat and skin that are result of rendering the fat from the skin of a pig. They're a delightful addition to cornbread. Slave cooks learned how to make all manner of breads and other nourishing dishes out of their ration of cornmeal. Frederick Douglass wrote about the disparity between the meals of slaves and the meals of their masters in his book, *The Life and Times of Frederick Douglass*, 1892.

"The close-fisted stinginess that fed the poor slave on coarse cornmeal and tainted meat...wholly vanished on approaching the sacred precincts of the Great House itself...immense wealth and its lavish expenditures filled the Great House with all that could please the eye and tempt the taste."

2 cups yellow cornmeal
1 1/2 teaspoons baking powder
1/2 teaspoon baking soda
1 1/2 teaspoons salt

1/2 cup cracklings
1 cup buttermilk
2 eggs, beaten
2 tablespoons bacon or ham drippings

1. Preheat the oven to 400 degrees. Sift together the cornmeal, baking powder, baking soda, and salt. Add the remaining ingredients and mix well. Spread the batter into an 8-inch baking dish. Bake 25 to 30 minutes.

Hoecakes

YIELD: ABOUT 14 CAKES

Many slaves devised a way to eat a hot meal in the short respite that was sometimes allowed at noontime. This "receipt" for hoecakes comes from a slave narrative collected by the Works Progress Administration in the 1940s. After you read it, you'll understand how these cornmeal cakes got their name.

"Stand in the shade near the edge of the field. Light a fire from whatever brush and twigs there may be. On the greased blade of your hoe, mix meal and water until it is thick enough to fry. Add salt, if you remembered to bring any. Lean the hoe into the fire until the top side of the bread bubbles. Flip it and brown the other side. If you do it without a hoe, you have to make suitable changes in the kitchen."

The following recipe makes "suitable changes in the kitchen."

2 cups white or yellow cornmeal
1/2 teaspoon salt
1 cup hot water

2 tablespoons melted vegetable shortening or bacon drippings, plus more for pan
1 to 1 1/2 cups cold water

1. In a bowl, combine the cornmeal, salt, hot water, and shortening. Add enough cold water to make the batter pour easily.

2. Grease a griddle or heavy skillet and set it over moderate heat. Pour about 2 tablespoons batter on the pan for each hoecake. After 3 to 5 minutes, or when the top begins to bubble, flip the hoecake with a spatula. Cook until the bottom turns a light brown. Eat immediately, as hoecakes lose their taste when reheated. Leftover cakes can be used in chicken stuffing.

Hush Puppies

YIELD: ABOUT 12 HUSH PUPPIES

Hush puppies are small, spicy balls of cornbread. They are rumored to have received their name when they were used to quiet hungry hunting dogs. A plate of fried fish seems mighty lonely without them.

1 cup white cornmeal
1/2 cup all-purpose flour
1/2 teaspoon salt
1 teaspoon sugar
1/2 teaspoon baking powder
1/2 teaspoon baking soda
1/2 teaspoon garlic powder

1/4 teaspoon cayenne pepper, or 2 or 3
   drops Tabasco sauce
2 scallions, including green tops, minced
1 egg, lightly beaten
Milk to moisten, up to 1 cup
2 cups bacon fat or vegetable oil

1. In a medium bowl, combine the cornmeal, flour, salt, sugar, baking powder, baking soda, garlic powder, cayenne pepper or Tabasco sauce, and scallions. Stir in the egg. Slowly add milk until the batter is thick but will drop easily from a teaspoon.

2. In a frying pan, heat the bacon fat or oil until hot enough for deep-fat frying. Drop the batter by teaspoonfuls into the fat and fry until golden, about 3 to 5 minutes, turning the hush puppies so they cook evenly. Repeat until all batter is used. Serve hot.

Pancakes

My mother said she always knew times were hard when pancakes were served for supper. Pancakes are delicious, simple to prepare, inexpensive, and filling—an especially good meal if you have nine children to feed, as my grandmother did.

2 cups milk

4 tablespoons (1/2 stick) butter, melted, plus extra for the pan

2 eggs, beaten

2 cups all-purpose flour

4 teaspoons baking powder

3 tablespoons sugar

1 teaspoon salt

1. In a bowl, combine the milk, butter, and eggs. Sift together the remaining ingredients and add to the milk mixture. Stir just until the ingredients are well combined.

2. Heat a skillet or griddle over moderate heat. Grease very lightly with butter. Drop the batter onto the skillet or griddle by 1/4 cupfuls. Cook, checking frequently, until the top side of the cake is full of bubbles and the underside is nicely browned. Turn the cake over and brown the other side. Repeat until all batter is used.

Spoon Bread

YIELD: 4 TO 6 SERVINGS

Spoon bread is light and rich, almost like a cornbread soufflé. It should be spooned up directly from the baking dish.

2 tablespoons butter, plus more for dish

2 cups whole milk

1/2 cup white cornmeal

1 teaspoon salt

1/2 teaspoon baking powder

2 eggs, separated

1. Preheat the oven to 400 degrees. Grease a 2-quart baking dish and put it in the oven to heat.

2. In a medium saucepan, bring the milk to a boil and gradually stir in the cornmeal; the mixture should be stiff. Add the salt and 2 tablespoons butter. Turn off the heat and stir in the baking powder. Lightly beat the egg yolks and stir them into the batter.

3. In a clean bowl, beat the egg whites until stiff, and fold into the batter. Pour the batter into the hot, greased baking dish. Bake 35 to 40 minutes, until the spoon bread is firm in the middle and brown on top.

Short'nin' Bread

YIELD: ABOUT 2 DOZEN (1 1/2-INCH) SQUARES

Mammy's little baby isn't the only one who loves short'nin' bread!

Vegetable oil cooking spray
2 cups all-purpose flour, sifted, plus more
 for dusting

1/2 cup packed light brown sugar
1 cup (2 sticks) butter, at room
 temperature

1. Preheat the oven to 350 degrees. Grease a cookie sheet lightly with cooking spray. Mix the flour, sugar, and butter until they form a soft dough. Dust a cutting board with flour and pat out the dough to a 1/2-inch thickness. With a knife, slice the dough into 1 1/2-inch squares. Place the squares on a lightly greased cookie sheet and bake for 10 to 12 minutes.

Desserts

Peach Cobbler

YIELD: 10 SERVINGS

My grandmother Willie Mae made "dumplings" for her peach cobbler out of leftover bits of pastry dough. She cooked the peach filling in a pot on the stove. When the peaches came to a boil, she dropped in the dumplings and then poured them into the crust to finish baking along with the rest of the cobbler. It was a delicious treat to spoon up the cinnamon-flavored dumplings along with the tasty peaches and crisp crust!

8 cups peeled, pitted, and sliced fresh peaches, or 8 cups frozen sliced peaches

12 tablespoons (1½ sticks) butter, plus more for dish

2 cups sugar

1½ teaspoons ground cinnamon

⅔ cup water

2 teaspoons fresh lemon juice

¼ cup all-purpose flour

Pastry for 3 (9-inch) piecrusts (page 250)

1. Preheat the oven to 350 degrees. Lightly butter a 9x13-inch baking dish. In a medium saucepan, combine all the ingredients except the flour and the piecrusts and bring to a boil. Simmer 5 to 10 minutes over low heat until the peaches are tender. Add a few tablespoons of the liquid from the peaches to the flour. Blend until smooth and stir the flour mixture into the saucepan.

2. Combine 2 pie pastries in a ball and roll out on a lightly floured board about ¼ inch thick. Put the pastry in the bottom of the prepared dish. Spoon in the peach mixture. On a lightly floured surface, roll the remaining pastry out ¼ inch thick and cut into ½-inch strips. Arrange the strips in a lattice over the peaches. Bake 35 to 45 minutes, or until the top is brown and the peaches are bubbling.

VARIATION FOR CANNED PEACHES

Using 2 (16-ounce) cans sliced peaches: Reduce the sugar to 1¼ cups, and follow the instructions for fresh peach cobbler, above. Simmer the filling mixture just enough to heat the peaches through, about 3 to 5 minutes.

Salt Pork Cakes

YIELD: 1 (10-INCH) SQUARE CAKE

I'm sure an ingenious African-American cook made do with her slave's ration of salt pork to concoct this moist, delicious cake. The salt pork was a substitute for shortening. This cake has the taste, denseness, and texture of a fruitcake or a spice cake without the eggs or candied fruit. It's easier to cut up the salt pork when it's slightly frozen.

1 tablespoon butter, for pan
3 cups all-purpose flour, plus more for pan
1 cup finely minced salt pork
1 cup boiling water
1 cup molasses
1/2 teaspoon baking soda

1 cup sugar
1 teaspoon ground cinnamon
1/2 teaspoon ground nutmeg
1/2 teaspoon ground cloves
1/2 teaspoon ground allspice
1 cup raisins

1. Grease and lightly flour a 10-inch square baking pan and set aside. Put the salt pork in a large mixing bowl. Pour the boiling water over the salt pork and let stand until cool. Pour the salt pork and the water into a food processor and blend until smooth. Preheat the oven to 350 degrees.

2. Add the molasses, baking soda, sugar, cinnamon, nutmeg, cloves, and allspice to the pork mixture. Blend until well combined and pour into a mixing bowl.

3. With a mixer on medium speed, beat 3 cups flour into the salt pork mixture 1 cup at a time until the mixture is smooth. Add the raisins. Pour into the baking pan. Bake 45 minutes, or until a toothpick inserted in the center of the cake comes out clean.

Michael's Lemon Chess Pie

YIELD: 1 (9-INCH) PIE

Chess pie is a very old and very popular dessert in the South. The ingredients are usually on hand, and it's simple to make. When my husband, Michael, has had a bad day this pie makes life sweet again.

4 eggs, at room temperature
8 tablespoons (1 stick) butter, softened
1½ cups sugar
1 tablespoon all-purpose flour

Pinch salt
2 tablespoons fresh lemon juice
1 teaspoon vanilla extract
1 unbaked 9-inch pie shell (page 250)

1. Preheat the oven to 325 degrees. Cream together the eggs and butter until fluffy, do not overbeat. Add the sugar, flour, and salt and mix well. Stir in the lemon juice and vanilla extract. Pour the filling into the pie shell and bake until the filling is set, about 35 minutes. Remove from the oven and allow the pie to firm as it cools. Serve chilled.

Sweet Potato Pie

YIELD: 6 SERVINGS

> The tater patch don't go on looks. —Slave proverb

2 cups boiled and mashed sweet potatoes
1¼ cups sugar
1 teaspoon lemon extract
1 tablespoon vanilla extract
1 teaspoon ground nutmeg

3 eggs
1 tablespoon cream
6 tablespoons butter
1 teaspoon all-purpose flour
1 unbaked 9-inch pie shell (page 250)

1. Preheat the oven to 350 degrees. With a mixer on medium speed, blend all the ingredients (except the pie shell) until smooth.

2. Spoon the filling into the unbaked pie shell. Bake 1 hour, or until firm except for a quarter-sized portion in the center. Allow the pie to cool for 2 hours before serving.

Rice Pudding

YIELD: 6 SERVINGS

> A smart redbird don't have much to say. —Slave proverb

½ cup raisins
2 cups milk
1½ cups cooked rice
2 eggs, beaten

1 teaspoon vanilla
½ cup sugar
½ teaspoon salt
¼ teaspoon ground nutmeg

1. Preheat the oven to 275 degrees. Fill the bottom of a double boiler with water and bring to a boil. In the top of the double boiler, combine the raisins and milk and cook, over medium heat, stirring often, 10 minutes, or until the raisins are soft. Add the rice and cook 5 minutes. Mix in the eggs, vanilla, sugar, salt, and nutmeg. Simmer another 5 minutes, then remove from the heat. Pour the pudding into a 1-quart ovenproof casserole. Bake 10 to 15 minutes.

Bread Pudding

YIELD: 6 SERVINGS

Nothing went to waste in an old-fashioned kitchen. Stale bread was dressed up with apples and turned into a tasty dessert.

1 tablespoon fresh lemon juice
1/2 cup packed brown sugar
4 sweet apples (Cortland, Pippin, Golden Delicious, Gala, or Rome), peeled, cored, and cubed
1 cup milk, scalded
2 eggs, beaten
1/4 cup granulated sugar

1/2 teaspoon ground nutmeg
1/2 teaspoon vanilla extract
1/2 cup raisins
2 tablespoons butter, melted, plus more for pan
8 slices stale white bread
1 cup bread crumbs

1. Preheat the oven to 350 degrees. In a medium mixing bowl, combine the lemon juice and 1/4 cup of the brown sugar. Add the apples and stir to coat. Refrigerate 1 hour.

2. In a large bowl, mix the milk, eggs, white sugar, nutmeg, vanilla extract, the remaining 1/4 cup brown sugar, the raisins, and the melted butter. Tear the bread into pieces and add it to the bowl. Mix well, mashing the bread. Add the apples and all the sugary liquid that has accumulated in the bowl with them to the bread mixture. Mix well.

3. Grease a 1-quart casserole or 9-inch square baking pan. Pour the mixture into the pan. Sprinkle with the bread crumbs. Cover with aluminum foil and bake 30 minutes. Uncover and bake 5 minutes longer, or until a knife stuck in the center comes out clean.

Tea Cakes

YIELD: ABOUT 2 DOZEN (3-INCH) CAKES

These cookies were my first introduction to Southern cooking—African-American style. There are many variations of the recipe, but I like this one.

8 tablespoons (1 stick) butter or margarine, plus more for pan
1 cup sugar, plus more for sprinkling the cakes
2 eggs, beaten
1 teaspoon vanilla extract

3 1/2 cups sifted all-purpose flour, plus more for dusting
1 teaspoon baking powder
1/2 teaspoon salt
1/2 teaspoon ground nutmeg
1/2 cup sour cream

1. In a large bowl, cream the butter and sugar until fluffy and well blended. Beat in the eggs and vanilla extract. In a separate bowl, sift together the flour, baking powder, salt, and nutmeg and add to the butter mixture, alternating with tablespoons of sour cream and mixing well. Wrap the dough in plastic or sheets of waxed paper and chill 4 hours or overnight.

2. Preheat the oven to 425 degrees. Grease a baking sheet with butter. Dust a cutting board with flour and roll out the dough 1/4 inch thick. Cut with a 3-inch round cookie cutter. Put the tea cakes on the baking sheet. Sprinkle with sugar. Bake 10 to 12 minutes, or until lightly browned.

Vinegar Pie

YIELD: 1 (9-INCH) PIE

Long ago, lemons weren't always affordable or available. Vinegar is a surprisingly good substitute.

3 egg yolks
1 cup sugar
1/4 cup all-purpose flour
1/3 teaspoon salt
2 cups boiling water
1/4 cup cider vinegar
1/2 teaspoon yellow food coloring
    (optional)
1 baked 9-inch pie shell (page 250)

MERINGUE:
3 egg whites
3 tablespoons sugar
1 teaspoon lemon extract
1/3 teaspoon salt

1. Preheat the oven to 325 degrees. Beat the egg yolks until thick. Add the sugar, flour, and salt and mix thoroughly. Gradually stir in the boiling water. Stir in the vinegar. Fill the bottom of a double boiler with water and bring to a boil; place the mixture in the top of the double boiler and cook the mixture until thickened, about 3 minutes. Stir in the food coloring, if desired, and pour into the baked pie shell.

2. Prepare the meringue: In a clean bowl, beat the egg whites, gradually adding the sugar 1 tablespoon at a time. Slowly beat in the lemon extract and salt. Beat until the meringue is stiff and glossy and stands in peaks when the beaters are removed.

3. Cover the pie with the meringue, being careful to seal all the edges. Bake 15 to 20 minutes, or until the meringue is golden brown.

Buttermilk Pound Cake

YIELD: 1 (10-INCH) TUBE CAKE

All the ingredients for this old-fashioned recipe should be at room temperature.

1 cup (2 sticks) butter, plus more for pan
3 cups sifted all-purpose flour, plus more
   for pan
1/2 teaspoon baking soda
1/2 teaspoon baking powder
3/4 teaspoon salt

2 cups sugar
5 eggs, separated
1 teaspoon grated lemon zest
1 teaspoon almond extract
1 cup buttermilk

1. Preheat the oven to 350 degrees. Butter and lightly flour a 10-inch tube pan and line the bottom of the pan with waxed or parchment paper. Sift together the flour, baking soda, baking powder, and salt; then sift again. Set aside.

2. Cream the butter until soft. Gradually beat in the sugar until the mixture is light and fluffy. Beat in the egg yolks 1 at a time until just mixed; do not overbeat. Add the lemon zest and almond extract. Beat in the flour mixture alternating with the buttermilk, starting and ending with the flour and beating well after each addition.

3. In a small bowl, beat the egg whites until light and fluffy but not dry. Fold the whites into the batter. Pour the batter into the tube pan. Bake about 1 hour, or until a toothpick inserted in the cake comes out clean. Cool the cake in the pan 5 minutes. Slide a knife around the interior rims of the pan. Turn the cake out onto a cake rack. Remove the paper carefully. Let the cake cool completely before serving.

Drinks

Sassafras Tea

YIELD: 6 SERVINGS

My grandmother Willie Mae often made tea from sassafras bark. My mother remembers how pretty and refreshing the coppery-red tea was on a hot summer's day after working in the field. When my father was a child, he was given sassafras tea whenever he had a cold or was feeling under the weather. Sassafras root is available in most natural-foods stores. The root can be used for several pots of tea, and becomes stronger each time it is boiled.

1 small bunch sassafras root, cut into
   chunks

6 to 8 cups water
2 tablespoons sugar or honey, to taste

1. Put the sassafras and water in a saucepan and boil until the tea is the desired strength, about 5 minutes. Sweeten to taste.

Old-Fashioned Molasses Nog

YIELD: 4 SERVINGS

Since there has been so much concern recently about ingesting raw eggs, I was happy to discover this old recipe for eggless "eggnog."

2 cups evaporated milk

2 cups ice-cold water

1/2 teaspoon salt

2 tablespoons sorghum molasses

Ground nutmeg, ginger, or cinnamon, for sprinkling

1. In a blender, blend the milk, water, salt, and molasses and pour into glasses. Sprinkle a little nutmeg, ginger, or cinnamon, or the spice of your choice, on top.

Hot Southern Cider

YIELD: 8 SERVINGS

Apple cider, whether served hot or cold, is an old-time favorite. This recipe makes the whole house smell wonderful. It's the perfect remedy for a cold, wintry day.

8 cups apple cider

12 whole cloves

1 teaspoon ground allspice

2 cinnamon sticks, broken into pieces

1. In a large saucepan over high heat, bring all the ingredients to a boil, stirring constantly. Remove from the heat as soon as the mixture comes to a boil. Strain through a fine sieve. Serve immediately.

"Divabetics"
Healthy Living for
a New Millenium

Divabetics

More than 3 million African-Americans have some type of diabetes. Three members of my immediate family have this disease. We call the women in my family who have diabetes "Divabetics." They maintain a positive "diva" attitude about their need to take care of their health. Attitude is everything when you're faced with health issues. The key to living a long and healthy life with any diet-related illness is to face the challenges and make the changes you need to make.

When you have diabetes you have to change the way you eat and the way you relate to food. This chapter provides recipes that are delicious, unique, and healthy, while taking the health issues of diabetics into consideration.

I hope that this chapter will provide you with a new way to look at food, modern meals, healthy eating, and taking care of yourself mentally, physically, and spiritually so that you can live life to the fullest. That's the philosophy I try to convey on The Kitchen Diva! in the hopes that the viewers who are watching me cook can take away something from the show that will enhance their lives.

At our house, we still prepare desserts, but we offer a variety of delicious and healthy choices to accommodate the needs of our family members and friends who are diabetic. You'll find some of the recipes my family loves in this chapter. If you've been diagnosed with diabetes or another health-related illness, take care of yourself and your health. It's the best thing you can do for yourself and the ones you love.

For information about the medical aspects of diabetes, including warning signs, check out www.divabetic.org and www.diabetes.org.

Condiments, Sauces, and Toppings

Blueberry Syrup

YIELD: 1 1/2 CUPS

If you haven't found a syrup designed for use by diabetics that you enjoy, this is a great, low-sugar recipe with the added benefit of the nutritious blueberries.

1 (12-ounce) bag unsweetened frozen
   blueberries, thawed
1/2 cup water
1 tablespoon butter

1/4 teaspoon nutmeg
1 tablespoon fresh lemon juice
4 teaspoons cornstarch
3 1/2 tablespoons sugar substitute

1. In a medium saucepan, combine the blueberries with 2 tablespoons of the water, the butter, nutmeg, and lemon juice. Bring the mixture to a boil, then reduce the heat to a simmer, stirring occasionally, until the berries are soft, about 8 to 10 minutes.

2. Dissolve the cornstarch in the remaining water. Add the cornstarch mixture to the blueberries and continue to cook, stirring constantly, until the syrup thickens, about 5 minutes. Remove the pan from the heat, and allow the syrup to cool, about 15 minutes. Stir in the sweetener. Store in an airtight container and refrigerate. Use within 7 days.

Peanut-Caramel Dip

YIELD: ABOUT 1/2 CUP

1/4 cup reduced-fat chunky peanut butter
2 tablespoons fat-free caramel ice cream
 topping

2 tablespoons fat-free milk
1 large apple, thinly sliced
4 large pretzel rods, broken in half

1. Combine the peanut butter, caramel topping, and milk in small saucepan. Heat over low heat, stirring constantly, until mixture is melted and warm. Serve dip with apple slices and pretzel rods.

2. Microwave directions: Combine all ingredients except apple slices and pretzel rods in a small microwavable dish. Microwave on medium (50%) 1 minute; stir well. Microwave an additional minute or until mixture is melted and warm.

Texas-Style Barbecue Sauce

YIELD: 1 1/3 CUPS

We love our "cueing sauce" here in Texas. This is a diabetic-friendly version that keeps the flavor and the spice.

1 (16-ounce) can tomato sauce
1/2 cup fresh lemon juice
1/4 cup apple-cider vinegar
2 tablespoons brown sugar substitute

2 teaspoons Dijon mustard
1 teaspoon cayenne pepper
1/2 teaspoon garlic powder

1. Combine all the ingredients in a medium, nonreactive saucepan and cook over high heat until the ingredients come to a boil, stirring constantly. Cover the pan and simmer 15 to 20 minutes on low heat, stirring occasionally. Store in an airtight container. The sauce can be used immediately, but for best results, refrigerate overnight to allow the flavors to meld.

Roasted Tomatillo Salsa

YIELD: 2 CUPS

Tomatillos look like a small green tomato with a papery outer skin that is removed and discarded. They have a very tart flavor, not at all like a tomato, and provide a unique flavor to this spicy salsa.

Olive oil cooking spray
8 fresh tomatillos, husks removed
1 jalapeño pepper, stem and seeds
   removed

1/2 onion, sliced
4 cloves garlic
Grated zest and juice of 1 lemon

1. Preheat the oven to 350 degrees. Spray a baking sheet lightly with the cooking spray. Place the tomatillos, jalapeño, onions, and garlic on the baking sheet. Lightly spritz with cooking spray. Roast 20 to 25 minutes, until the garlic is golden and soft.

2. Transfer the vegetables to a food processor. Process until smooth. Add the lemon zest and juice. Pulse again to mix. Store in an airtight container and refrigerate.

Yogurt Topping

YIELD: ABOUT 1 CUP

If you love sour cream or cream cheese, but need to trim calories, this thickened yogurt "cheese" is the one for you. Straining out the whey thickens the yogurt and makes it a delicious substitute for more fattening cheeses. Adding fresh herbs gives this simple spread a French Boursin cheese flavor. This is also great as a topping for a baked potato.

2 cups plain, low-fat, no gelatin added, yogurt

1. Line a sieve with a coffee filter or 2 layers of cheesecloth. Suspend the sieve over a deep bowl. Scrape the yogurt into the filter and refrigerate for several hours or overnight to allow the whey to drain out until the yogurt is the texture of a soft cream cheese. Transfer the yogurt out of the filter, discarding the liquid in the bowl. Place the yogurt topping into an airtight plastic container and refrigerate. The yogurt topping will keep for a week. Drain off any liquid that might have accumulated before using.

Appetizers and Snacks

Tuna Baguette

YIELD: 6 SERVINGS

If you're trying to eat a healthier lunch, this sandwich is the perfect solution, because you can make it in advance and it tastes even better the next day.

1 large French baguette, about 1 pound

4 tomatoes, peeled and chopped

4 scallions, white and green parts, finely chopped

1 green bell pepper, seeded and chopped

1 (6-ounce) can water-packed tuna, drained and flaked

1 tablespoon dill pickle relish

3 tablespoons red wine vinegar

2 tablespoons olive oil

1 teaspoon Dijon mustard

1 clove garlic, minced

2 tablespoons chopped parsley

1 tablespoon chopped fresh mint, or 1 teaspoon dried

1 teaspoon fresh thyme leaves, or 1/4 teaspoon dried

1. Cut the baguette in half horizontally and scoop out some of the bread to create a shell. Reserve the crumbs from the inside of the bread.

2. In a large bowl, combine the tomatoes, scallions, bell pepper, tuna, dill pickle relish, and the reserved bread crumbs.

3. In a small bowl, whisk together the vinegar, oil, mustard, garlic, parsley, mint, and thyme. Drizzle the dressing over the tuna mixture and toss to mix thoroughly. Mound the mixture into the bottom half of the bread, packing down firmly. Top with the other half of the bread. Press bread halves together and wrap tightly in plastic wrap or aluminum foil. Refrigerate for several hours or overnight to allow the flavors to develop. To serve, cut into 6 portions.

Veggie Dip

YIELD: 6 SERVINGS

This nutrition-packed dip is high in protein and uses the creamy, soft type of tofu to perfection. It also makes a great spread for sandwiches and wraps. It's a great snack and a wonderful way to eat your vegetables!

1 block soft, silken tofu, drained (8 ounces)
1 (4-ounce) package ranch dressing mix
1/4 cup finely chopped carrots
1/4 cup finely chopped cucumbers
1/4 cup finely chopped red bell peppers
1/4 cup finely chopped zucchini
2 scallions, white and green tops, chopped

1. Combine the tofu and dressing mix in blender; mix well.

2. Scrape the tofu mixture into a small bowl with an airtight cover. Stir in the chopped vegetables. Cover and refrigerate 2 to 3 hours for flavors to blend. Serve with assorted fresh vegetable dippers or baked pita chips.

Baked Sweet Potato Thins

YIELD: 4 SERVINGS

Olive oil or canola oil cooking spray
2 (8-ounce) sweet potatoes, peeled and very thinly sliced
1 teaspoon salt
1 teaspoon black pepper, or to taste

1. Preheat the oven to 375 degrees. Spray a nonstick cookie sheet with cooking spray. Heat the cookie sheet in the oven until hot, about 5 minutes.

2. Carefully place the potato slices in a single layer on the sheet pan and spray with the cooking spray. Sprinkle with the salt and pepper.

3. Bake, turning once if necessary, until the potatoes are cooked through. The time will depend on the thickness, 10 to 15 minutes.

Nacho Bell Peppers

YIELD: 4 SERVINGS

Want to add a little spice to your appetizers without adding calories? This veggie version of Mexican nachos is tasty, quick, and healthy!

1 green bell pepper
1 yellow or red bell pepper
1 tablespoon olive oil
2 Italian plum tomatoes, seeded and
  finely chopped
1 cup finely chopped onion
1 teaspoon chili powder
1 teaspoon ground cumin

1 cup cooked white or brown rice
1/4 cup (2 ounces) shredded reduced-fat
  Monterey Jack or pepper Jack cheese
1/4 cup chopped fresh cilantro
1/4 teaspoon Tabasco sauce
1/4 cup (2 ounces) shredded reduced-fat
  sharp cheddar cheese
Vegetable oil cooking spray

1. Cut bell peppers into 2x1 1/2-inch strips; cut strips into bite-size triangles (each strip should yield 2 or 3 triangles). Spray a large baking sheet with cooking spray. Place the bell pepper triangles on the baking sheet and set aside.

2. Add the olive oil to a large nonstick skillet. Add the tomatoes, onion, chili powder, and cumin. Cook over medium heat 3 minutes, or until the onion is tender, stirring occasionally. Remove the pan from the heat. Stir in the rice, Monterey Jack cheese, cilantro, and Tabasco.

3. Top each pepper triangle with about 2 tablespoons rice mixture; sprinkle with the cheddar cheese. Cover the pepper triangles on the baking sheets with plastic wrap. Refrigerate 1 hour or up to 8 hours before serving.

4. When ready to serve, preheat the broiler. Remove plastic wrap. Broil the nachos 6 to 8 inches from the heat, watching carefully to prevent burning, 3 to 4 minutes (or bake at 400 degrees 8 to 10 minutes) until the cheese is bubbly and the rice is heated through.

Tex-Mex Onion Rings

YIELD: MAKES 6 SERVINGS

I love onion rings, but I don't love the extra calories that frying adds on to the finished dish. These crispy oven-fried onion rings are guaranteed to satisfy your snack food cravings. This recipe can also be used to coat strips of chicken breast or pieces of fish.

Vegetable oil cooking spray
1 cup bread crumbs
1/2 cup yellow cornmeal
11/2 teaspoons chili powder
11/2 teaspoons salt
11/2 teaspoons black pepper

1/8 teaspoon cayenne pepper, or to taste
11/2 tablespoons butter, melted
1 teaspoon water
2 onions (sweet variety, such as Vidalia),
    sliced into rings, 3/8 inch thick
2 egg whites

1. Preheat the oven to 450 degrees. Cover a large baking pan with aluminum foil and spray the foil with cooking spray. Place the pan in the oven to get hot.

2. Combine the bread crumbs, cornmeal, 1/2 teaspoon of the chili powder, 1/2 teaspoon of the salt, 1/2 teaspoon of the black pepper, and the cayenne pepper in a medium shallow dish, mixing the ingredients well to combine them. Stir in the melted butter and the water.

3. Separate the onion slices into rings. Place the egg whites, the remaining 1 teaspoon each chili powder, salt, and black pepper into a large bowl, beating the whites lightly. Add the onion rings, tossing lightly to coat them evenly. Dredge the coated rings in the bread crumb mixture, toss to coat evenly, and place the rings in a single layer on the preheated baking sheet. Spray the rings with the cooking spray. Bake 12 to 15 minutes, or until the onions are tender and the coating is crisp.

Pizza Pockets

YIELD: 8 SERVINGS

8 ounces ground white meat chicken or
   lean ground beef
1 onion, chopped (about 1 cup)
2 large cloves garlic, smashed
1 cup grated zucchini, or chopped broccoli
1 (7$1/2$-ounce) can tomato sauce
$1/2$ teaspoon dried oregano
1 teaspoon dried basil
$1/4$ teaspoon black pepper
$1/4$ teaspoon crushed red pepper flakes
$3/4$ cup part-skim mozzarella cheese

$1/4$ cup grated Parmesan cheese
Vegetable oil cooking spray

PIZZA DOUGH:
$2/3$ cup whole wheat flour
$11/3$ cups all-purpose flour
4 teaspoons baking powder
$1/2$ teaspoon salt
3 tablespoons canola oil
1 cup skim milk
Cornmeal, for dusting

1. Preheat the oven to 400 degrees. Sauté the chicken or beef, the onion, garlic, and zucchini in a large nonstick frying pan until no pink remains in the meat and the liquid is evaporated. Stir in the tomato sauce, oregano, basil, black pepper, and red pepper flakes. Simmer, uncovered, on low for 10 minutes until thickened. Remove from the heat. Let cool slightly, 3 to 5 minutes, then stir in the cheeses. Set aside.

2. To make the pizza dough: Combine the whole wheat flour, 1 cup of the all-purpose flour, the baking powder, and salt in a large bowl. Make a well in the center of the flour and set aside.

3. Combine the canola oil and $3/4$ cup of the milk in a small bowl. Add the milk mixture to the center of the dry ingredients and stir with a fork until just moistened and the mixture begins to form a dough. Turn the dough out onto a lightly floured board add the remaining $1/3$ cup all-purpose flour.

4. Gently knead the dough 8 to 10 times. Divide the dough into 8 portions and roll each out to a 6-inch circle. Place $1/3$ cup meat filling to one side of the center of each circle. Moisten the edge of the dough with some of the remaining milk. Bring the unfilled side of dough up and over the filling. Press the edges of the dough together firmly with the tines of a fork to seal. Cut a few slits in the top of each pizza pocket with the tip of a sharp knife. Spray the cooking spray on the baking sheet and sprinkle the cornmeal all over the sheet pan. Place the pizza pockets on the baking sheet. Brush the tops with the remaining milk. Bake 15 to 18 minutes, until golden brown.

Peanut Butter Granola

YIELD: 6 SERVINGS

3 cups rolled oats
1/2 cup wheat germ
1/2 cup smooth natural peanut butter

1 1/2 tablespoons light brown sugar
1/3 cup raisins

1. Preheat the oven to 300 degrees. In a medium bowl, combine the oats and the wheat germ. Place the peanut butter and brown sugar in a microwave-safe dish. Mix well. Microwave on high 20 seconds, until warm. Stir again.

2. Pour the peanut butter mixture over the cereal and toss to coat evenly. Stir in the raisins.

3. Spread the granola evenly in a baking pan and bake 20 minutes, stirring once. Cool before serving. Store the granola in resealable plastic bags. Eat within 2 days.

Drinks

Blueberry Fizz

YIELD: 1 SERVING

This is a refreshing drink that's high on taste and low on sugar.

1/4 cup unsweetened frozen blueberries
1/4 cup skim milk

1/2 cup club soda, chilled
2 teaspoons sugar substitute

1. In a blender, whirl all ingredients until smooth. Serve in a tall glass.

Cinnamon Cafe au Lait

YIELD: 1 SERVING

This delicious drink is easy to prepare. Cinnamon, according to some studies, may improve blood glucose and cholesterol levels in people with type 2 diabetes.

1 cup skim milk
1 teaspoon sugar substitute

1/4 to 1/2 teaspoon cinnamon
1 teaspoon instant coffee granules

1. In small saucepan, mix the milk, sugar substitute, and cinnamon and simmer over medium-low heat. Place the instant coffee granules into a coffee cup. Pour the milk mixture into the coffee cup and stir well.

Diabetic "Champagne"

YIELD: 6 CUPS

This nonalcoholic drink for diabetics is festive anytime.

4 cups white grape juice
2 cups diet lemon-lime soda
1/2 cup sugar substitute

Strawberries, for garnish (optional)
Lemon or lime slices, for garnish (optional)

1. In a large bowl, mix the grape juice, soda, and sugar substitute together. Refrigerate. Stir chilled ingredients together just before serving. Garnish with fruit, if desired.

Spiced Tomato Juice

YIELD: 6 SERVINGS

This is a refreshing way to start off a hot summer day!

1 (46-ounce) can reduced-sodium
   tomato juice
1/2 teaspoon onion powder
1/2 teaspoon celery seeds
1/2 teaspoon dried basil

1/4 tablespoon artificial sweetener
2 tablespoons white vinegar
5 to 6 drops Tabasco sauce (optional)
Celery stalks, for garnish

1. Mix tomato juice, onion powder, celery seeds, basil, artificial sweetener, and vinegar together and chill. Add Tabasco sauce before serving, if desired. Place celery stalks in the glass for garnish.

Starters

Baked Apple Frittata

YIELD: 4 SERVINGS

Butter-flavored cooking spray
1¹/₂ cups egg substitute
¹/₃ cup low-fat (1%) milk
¹/₄ cup unbleached all-purpose flour
2 large Granny Smith apples, cored, thinly
    sliced, and sprinkled with fresh lemon
    juice

2 tablespoons packed brown sugar
    substitute
1 teaspoon vanilla
1 teaspoon cinnamon

1. Preheat the oven to 425 degrees. Lightly coat a 3-quart ovenproof pan with cooking spray. In a large bowl, whisk together the egg substitute, milk, and flour. Pour into prepared pan.

2. Toss the apple slices with the brown sugar substitute, vanilla, and cinnamon. Arrange the apple slices in the batter and bake until frittata is puffed, golden brown, and set in center when pan is gently shaken, 8 to 10 minutes. Remove the frittata from the oven and allow to set, 5 minutes. Cut into wedges to serve.

Chicken Sausage Strata

YIELD: 8 SERVINGS

Chicken sausages come in a variety of flavors and make this a deliciously different way to start the day. You can prepare this dish the day before, so there's no reason not to have a great breakfast!

1 pound chicken sausage, casings removed
1/2 medium onion, diced
2 cloves garlic, diced
2 cups low-fat (1%) milk
11/2 cups egg substitute
Olive oil cooking spray

8 slices good-quality white bread, crusts removed and cut into cubes
3/4 cup shredded low-fat sharp cheddar cheese
11/2 cups salsa

1. In a nonstick skillet over medium heat, sauté the sausage, onion, and garlic until evenly browned, stirring and breaking up any large clumps with a wooden spoon. Using a slotted spoon, transfer the mixture to food-safe paper towels to thoroughly drain.

2. In a small bowl, whisk together the milk and egg substitute. Lightly coat a 2-quart casserole dish with cooking spray. Layer 1/3 of the bread cubes on the bottom of the prepared baking dish. Top with half of the browned sausage and 1/4 cup shredded cheese. Pour 1 cup of the milk-egg mixture over the top. Repeat the layers, finishing with the final bread layer and the remaining 11/2 cups of the milk-egg mixture. Cover with the salsa. Cover with plastic wrap and refrigerate overnight.

3. Preheat the oven to 350 degrees. Uncover the casserole. Sprinkle the top with the remaining 1/4 cup shredded cheese. Bake until the strata is bubbling and golden brown, and a knife inserted in the center comes out clean, 50 to 60 minutes. Remove from the oven and let sit for 10 minutes before serving.

Potato Omelet

YIELD: 16 SERVINGS

This hearty oven-baked omelet can be reheated and used as a filling in a whole-wheat tortilla, in pita bread, or on a bagel for breakfast the next day.

2 pounds russet potatoes, peeled and diced
Olive oil cooking spray
1 tablespoon olive oil
2 medium white onions, thinly sliced
3 large cloves garlic, minced
2 tablespoons chopped parsley

1 teaspoon black pepper
1 teaspoon salt
1/8 teaspoon cayenne pepper
1 1/2 cups liquid egg substitute or 6 large eggs, well beaten
1/2 cup low-fat sharp cheddar or Monterey Jack cheese

1. Microwave the potatoes in a large bowl 5 to 8 minutes on high until slightly soft when pierced with a knife in the center. Drain any liquid from the potatoes.

2. Place a 10-inch ovenproof pan over medium-high heat and coat with olive oil spray. Add the potatoes and onion; cook stirring frequently, until the potatoes are tender and the onion is golden brown. Stir in the garlic, parsley, black pepper, salt, and cayenne pepper. Cook, stirring, another 5 minutes.

3. Transfer the potato mixture to a large bowl. Mix in egg substitute. Preheat the broiler.

4. Wipe out the skillet with paper towels and recoat it with a little olive oil. Add the potato-egg mixture to the skillet and cook over low heat, pressing the potatoes down with a pancake turner so that they are completely covered by the egg. Cook, covered, until the egg on the sides of the skillet is slightly brown and the egg mixture starts to set, about 10 minutes. Place the omelet under the broiler until the center is cooked through, the top is golden brown, 3 to 5 minutes.

5. Place a large serving dish over the skillet. Carefully invert the omelet onto the serving dish, sprinkle with cheese, and cool to room temperature. Cut into very small wedges.

Homemade Turkey Sausage

YIELD: 6 SERVINGS

1/4 onion, minced
3 tablespoons quick rolled oats
2 teaspoons dried parsley
1 teaspoon salt
1/2 teaspoon ground sage
1/4 teaspoon ground cloves
1/4 teaspoon ground nutmeg

1 teaspoon black pepper
1/8 teaspoon cayenne pepper
1 egg white
1/2 pound ground white or mixed
   (white and dark) turkey meat
Vegetable oil cooking spray

1. In a small mixing bowl, combine the onion, oats, parsley, salt, sage, cloves, nutmeg, black pepper and cayenne pepper until well mixed.

2. In a medium mixing bowl, beat the egg white with a fork and combine with the turkey. Add in the spice mixture. Spray a large skillet with vegetable oil spray and preheat over medium heat. Shape the turkey mixture into 8 patties and cook 12 to 15 minutes, turning once.

Salads and Side Dishes

Mango Chicken Salad

YIELD: 6 SERVINGS

2 cups diced cooked boneless skinless
    chicken breasts
1 large mango, peeled and cut into
    1/2-inch cubes
1/2 cup halved green grapes
1/2 cup celery
1/4 cup minced red onions
2 tablespoons minced scallions

2 teaspoons minced parsley
1 cup fat-free mayonnaise
2 tablespoons low-fat sour cream
1 tablespoon fresh orange juice
1/4 teaspoon ground ginger
1 teaspoon salt
1 teaspoon black pepper
Lettuce greens, for serving

1. In a large salad bowl, combine the chicken, mango, grapes, celery, red onions, scallions, and parsley. In a small bowl, whisk together the mayonnaise, sour cream, orange juice, ginger, salt, and black pepper. Fold the dressing into the chicken salad. Cover and chill for 1 hour. Serve on a bed of lettuce greens.

Dilled Cucumbers and Onions

YIELD: 8 SERVINGS

9 cucumbers, about 21/2 pounds
1 red onion, halved and sliced
1 tablespoon chopped fresh dill
1 teaspoon salt

1 teaspoon black pepper
1 teaspoon celery seeds
1/3 cup cider vinegar
1/4 cup olive oil

1. Run the tines of a fork from top to bottom of each cucumber, working your way around the entire cucumber. Slice the cucumbers into thick rounds. Put the cucumbers and onion in a large mixing bowl, and toss with the dill, salt, black pepper, and celery seeds. Let stand 30 minutes.

2. Stir in the vinegar and oil. Refrigerate until ready to serve. Serve as a bed or a topping for fish fillets.

Shrimp Salad with Corn and Peaches

YIELD: 4 SERVINGS

3 ears fresh corn, kernels removed from the cob, or 1 cup frozen, thawed corn kernels

1 jarred roasted red bell pepper, drained and coarsely chopped

1 small white onion, chopped

1/4 medium jicama, peeled and julienned

1/4 teaspoon cumin

1 clove garlic, minced

2 tablespoons olive oil

2 tablespoons fresh lime juice

1 fresh jalapeño pepper, seeded and finely minced

1 pound peeled, cooked large shrimp

2 large ripe peaches or 2 cups frozen, thawed, and drained peaches

1 head radicchio, romaine, or butter lettuce, separated into leaves, for serving

1/4 cup minced cilantro

1 teaspoon black pepper

1 teaspoon salt

1. If using fresh corn, in a medium pot of boiling water, blanch the corn kernels 2 minutes. Drain and refresh under running cold water. Put the corn in a large bowl. Add the roasted pepper, onion, and jicama.

2. In a small bowl, whisk to combine the cumin, garlic, olive oil, lime juice, and jalapeño.

3. Lay the shrimp in a shallow dish and pour on the cumin–olive oil mixture. Toss to coat. Wash and peel the peaches (if necessary, dip the peaches in boiling water for 1 minute to facilitate removing the skin) and cut in half; remove the pits. Slice into wedges and add to the salad bowl. Or use frozen peaches that have been thawed and drained.

4. When ready to serve, arrange 2 or 3 radicchio, romaine, or butter lettuce leaves on individual dinner plates. Toss the corn-peach mixture and spoon onto the leaves. Arrange the shrimp over the salad and spoon on any remaining dressing. Sprinkle with the cilantro and season with black pepper and salt.

Diva-style Waldorf Salad

YIELD: 4 SERVINGS

This Waldorf salad is an elegant recipe that I've updated for modern times.

1 teaspoon fresh lemon juice
2 1/2 cups diced apples (Gala, Granny
   Smith, or Fuji)
1 cup diced celery strips
1/2 cup broken walnuts

1 tablespoon sugar substitute
1 teaspoon salt
1/2 cup low-fat vanilla yogurt
2 tablespoons low-fat mayonnaise
Lettuce leaves, for serving

1. Drizzle the lemon juice over the diced apples and toss well. Mix in the celery and walnuts. In a separate bowl, combine the sugar substitute, salt, yogurt, and mayonnaise.

2. Fold the yogurt mixture into the apple mixture. Chill, then serve on the lettuce leaves.

Coleslaw

YIELD: 6 SERVINGS

1/2 cup nonfat plain yogurt
2 tablespoons Dijon mustard
1 tablespoon fresh lemon juice
1 tablespoon fat-free mayonnaise
1 pound packaged shredded cabbage
   for coleslaw mix

1 teaspoon onion powder
1/2 teaspoon dried dill weed
1 teaspoon salt
1 teaspoon black pepper

1. In a large bowl, combine the yogurt, mustard, lemon juice, and mayonnaise.

2. Add the coleslaw mix and toss to coat. Sprinkle with onion powder, dill weed, salt, and black pepper. Mix well. Cover and refrigerate for up to 1 day before serving.

Main Course Meals

Fish Veronique

YIELD: 4 SERVINGS

Healthy eating doesn't mean boring food. This delicious dish is perfect for company.

Vegetable oil cooking spray
1 pound white fish fillets (tilapia, cod,
    sole, turbot, etc.)
1 teaspoon salt
1 teaspoon black pepper
1 teaspoon poultry seasoning
1/2 cup chicken broth

1 tablespoon fresh lemon juice
1 tablespoon butter, softened
1 tablespoon olive oil
2 tablespoons all-purpose flour
3/4 cup skim milk or low-fat (1%) milk
1/2 cup seedless grapes

1. Preheat the oven to 350 degrees. Spray a 10x6-inch baking dish with cooking spray. Place the fish in the pan and sprinkle with the salt, pepper, and poultry seasoning. Mix the broth and lemon juice in a small bowl and pour the mixture over the fish; cover. Bake 15 minutes.

2. Melt the butter and oil in a small saucepan. Remove from the heat and stir in the flour. Gradually stir in the milk, return the pan to the heat, and cook over moderately low heat, stirring constantly until thickened. Remove the fish from the oven and pour the liquid from the baking dish into the cream sauce, stirring until blended. Pour the sauce over the fish and sprinkle with grapes. Broil about 4 inches from the heat, until the sauce starts to brown, about 5 minutes.

Caribbean Chicken Stir-Fry

YIELD: 4 SERVINGS

4 (5-ounce) boneless and skinless chicken
    breast halves, trimmed of all visible fat
1 teaspoon ground coriander
1 teaspoon ground ginger
1 teaspoon paprika
1 teaspoon black pepper
1/2 teaspoon cayenne pepper
Grated zest of 1 lime
1 tablespoon olive oil
1/2 large yellow onion, thinly sliced
3 large cloves garlic, thinly sliced
4 scallions, trimmed leaving 2 inches
    green, cut lengthwise into thin strips

1 large red bell pepper, cored, seeded,
    and julienned
1 tablespoon minced ginger
1/2 teaspoon grated orange zest
1/4 cup fresh orange juice
2 tablespoons fresh lime juice
1 tablespoon cornstarch
2 tablespoons Caribbean-style
    Pickapeppa sauce
1/4 teaspoon ground allspice
1/8 teaspoon ground nutmeg

1. Rinse the chicken breasts and pat dry with paper towels. Cut crosswise into 1/2-inch-wide strips. In a large bowl, combine the coriander, ginger, paprika, black pepper, cayenne pepper, and lime zest. Add chicken strips and toss to evenly coat. Set aside for 15 minutes.

2. In a wok or heavy nonstick skillet over high heat, heat 1/2 tablespoon of the oil. When hot add onion, garlic, scallions, bell pepper, and minced ginger. Stir-fry 2 to 3 minutes. Transfer vegetables to a small bowl.

3. Add the remaining 1/2 tablespoon oil to the wok and place over medium-high heat. Add seasoned chicken breast strips and stir-fry 2 to 3 minutes.

4. Meanwhile, in a small bowl, whisk together the orange zest and juice, lime juice, cornstarch, Pickapeppa sauce, allspice, and nutmeg. Return the vegetables to the wok and stir in the sauce. Continue stir-frying for another minute or 2 until the sauce has thickened. Serve hot, over a bed of rice.

Turkey Patties with Curried Corn Pudding

YIELD: 4 SERVINGS

Turkey is often thought of as bland. This recipe infuses the meat with flavor, and the curried corn pudding is a delicious new twist on an old African-American recipe.

1 pound ground turkey (breast meat or mixed dark and white)
1 small onion, chopped
1/4 cup egg substitute
2 tablespoons dry bread crumbs
1 teaspoon ground thyme
1 teaspoon fennel seeds
1/2 teaspoon garlic powder

1/4 teaspoon salt
1/2 teaspoon black pepper
1/8 teaspoon cayenne pepper
1/4 teaspoon prepared horseradish
Vegetable oil cooking spray
Curried corn pudding (see following recipe)
2 tablespoons chopped flat leaf parsley

1. Combine the turkey, onion, egg substitute, bread crumbs, thyme, fennel, garlic powder, salt, black pepper, cayenne pepper, and horseradish in a large bowl and mix well. Do not overwork the meat. Form the mixture into 4 equal-sized patties.

2. Coat a large skillet with cooking spray and place the pan over medium heat. Cook the patties in the skillet 3 to 4 minutes per side, or until no pink remains in the center. Place an individual serving of the curried corn pudding in the center of a dinner plate. Place a turkey patty on top of the curried corn pudding. Sprinkle with the parsley.

Curried Corn Pudding

YIELD: 4 SERVINGS

Butter-flavored cooking spray
4 scallions, white parts only, minced
1 clove garlic, minced
1 1/2 teaspoons good-quality curry powder
1 1/2 cups fresh or frozen corn

3/4 cup evaporated skim milk
2 1/2 tablespoons chopped cilantro
2 teaspoons cornstarch
Juice of 1/2 lime

1. Preheat the oven to 350 degrees. Coat a small nonstick skillet with cooking spray and place the pan over medium-high heat. Sauté the scallion and garlic 4 minutes, until wilted. Add the curry powder and sauté 1 minute. Remove the pan from the heat.

2. Coat an 8-inch ovenproof dish with cooking spray. In a bowl, combine the corn, milk, cilantro, cornstarch, and lime juice. Stir in the scallion mixture. Pour the corn mixture into the prepared dish. Bake until the center is puffed and golden, about 30 minutes.

Pork Chops with Spicy Plums

YIELD: 4 SERVINGS

Vegetable oil cooking spray
3 tablespoons fresh lemon juice
3 scallions, thinly sliced
3 cloves garlic, minced
1 1/2 teaspoons dried rosemary, crushed
1 teaspoon salt
1 teaspoon black pepper
4 (6-ounce) pork chops
4 plums

1/2 cup unsweetened pineapple juice or apple juice
2 tablespoons packed brown sugar substitute
1/2 teaspoon cinnamon
1/4 teaspoon cardamom
1/8 teaspoon cumin
1 pinch nutmeg

1. Preheat the oven to 400 degrees. Coat an 8-inch square baking dish with cooking spray.

2. Combine the lemon juice, scallions, garlic, rosemary, salt, and black pepper in a shallow dish. Dip each pork chop into the mixture to coat completely, then place the chops in the baking dish. Lightly coat the chops with the cooking spray; set aside.

3. Cut each plum in half and remove the pits. Place plums in the baking pan around the pork chops, cut side up. Combine the fruit juice, the brown sugar substitute, and the spices in a small bowl. Drizzle spiced juice over the plums and the chops. Bake 15 to 20 minutes, or until the plums are tender and the chops are at the desired doneness.

Apple-Cherry Glazed Pork Chops

YIELD: 4 SERVINGS

1 teaspoon salt

1 teaspoon black pepper

1 tablespoon poultry seasoning

1/8 teaspoon cayenne pepper

4 (3-ounce) boneless pork loin chops,
   trimmed of fat

Olive oil cooking spray

2/3 cup unsweetened apple juice

1/2 small apple, sliced (Granny Smith,
   Gala, or Fuji)

2 scallions, thinly sliced

2 tablespoons dried tart cherries

1 teaspoon cornstarch

1 tablespoon water

1. Sprinkle the salt, black pepper, poultry seasoning, and cayenne pepper on the chops. Rub the seasonings onto both sides. Spray a large skillet with cooking spray. Place skillet over medium heat until hot. Add the pork chops to the pan and cook over medium heat 3 to 5 minutes or until barely pink in center, turning once. Remove the chops to a plate, cover with a sheet of foil, and set aside.

2. Add the apple juice, apple slices, scallions, and cherries to the same skillet. Simmer, uncovered, 2 to 3 minutes or until apples and scallions are tender. Combine the cornstarch and the water in a small bowl and stir into the skillet. Bring the ingredients to a boil and cook, stirring, until thickened. Spoon the sauce over the pork chops.

Breads and Desserts

Sweet Potato Biscuits

YIELD: 18 BISCUITS

Roasted sweet potatoes work best in this recipe. It's the perfect way to use leftovers and a great way to start the day.

Butter-flavored cooking spray or baking parchment paper

2 1/2 cups sifted unbleached all-purpose flour, plus more for dusting

2 tablespoons brown sugar substitute

2 teaspoons baking powder

1 teaspoon baking soda

1/2 teaspoon ground nutmeg

1/2 teaspoon salt

1/2 teaspoon sugar substitute

1/4 cup canola oil

3/4 cup plus 2 tablespoons nonfat buttermilk

3/4 cup cooked, mashed sweet potato

1. Preheat the oven to 425 degrees. Lightly spray a nonstick baking sheet with cooking spray or line with parchment paper. In a large bowl, combine the flour, brown sugar substitute, baking powder, baking soda, nutmeg, salt, and sugar substitute.

2. In a large measuring cup, combine the oil, buttermilk, and mashed sweet potato. Add the wet ingredients to the dry ingredients and mix until just combined; the dough will be quite dry.

3. Transfer the dough to a floured work surface. Knead a few times and pat to a 1-inch-thick rectangle about 8x5 inches. Dip a sharp knife in the flour, then cut the dough into thirds lengthwise. Then cut each long strip into 6 equal pieces, making 18 squares in all. Transfer the biscuits to the prepared baking sheet.

4. Bake 12 to 13 minutes, until the tops are golden and firm to the touch. Serve warm.

Quick Lemon Bread

YIELD: 10 SERVINGS

I love serving a light, lemony dessert after a spicy meal. This bread is perfect and tastes even better with a dollop of light whipped cream.

Vegetable oil cooking spray
1 cup sugar substitute
8 tablespoons (1 stick) butter, softened
1/2 cup egg whites, lightly beaten
1 1/2 cups all-purpose flour

1 teaspoon baking powder
1/2 teaspoon salt
1/2 cup skim milk
1 1/2 teaspoons grated lemon peel

1. Preheat the oven to 350 degrees. Spray a 5x9-inch loaf pan with cooking spray. In a large bowl, mix the sugar substitute, butter, and egg whites until smooth. Add the remaining ingredients and mix until the flour is incorporated into the batter. Pour the batter into the prepared pan. Bake 45 to 50 minutes, until a toothpick inserted in the center comes out clean.

2. Let the bread cool in the pan on a rack for 15 minutes, then turn the bread out onto the rack to cool.

Oatmeal-Raisin Cookies

YIELD: 1 DOZEN COOKIES

There's no reason why you can't have a cookie because of health issues, especially if they've been made with less-fattening ingredients.

1 cup all-purpose flour

1 1/2 teaspoons baking powder

1/2 teaspoon salt

1/4 teaspoon cinnamon

8 tablespoons (1 stick) butter, softened

2 tablespoons sugar substitute

1/3 cup brown sugar substitute

1 egg

2 tablespoons milk

1/2 teaspoon vanilla

1 1/2 cups quick oats

1/2 cup dark raisins

1. Preheat the oven to 325 degrees. Combine the flour, baking powder, salt, and cinnamon. Cream the butter and both sugar substitutes until fluffy. Mix in the egg, milk, and vanilla. Gradually mix in the flour mixture. Stir in the oats and raisins.

2. Cover a baking sheet with parchment paper. Drop the dough by teaspoonfuls if small cookies are desired (or tablespoonfulls if larger cookies are desired) onto the prepared pan. Bake until golden brown, 10 to 12 minutes. Cool on wire racks.

Banana Bran Pancakes with Vanilla Butter

YIELD: 4 SERVINGS

Topping these wonderful pancakes with vanilla butter eliminates the need for syrup.

1 1/3 cups skim milk

1/2 cup egg substitute

1 tablespoon vegetable oil

1 teaspoon vanilla

3/4 cup ripe mashed bananas

1 1/2 cups Multi-Bran Chex

1 cup all-purpose flour

3 tablespoons sugar substitute

1 teaspoon baking powder

1/2 teaspoon baking soda

1/4 teaspoon salt

1/4 teaspoon ground nutmeg

Vegetable oil cooking spray

Vanilla butter (see following recipe)

1. In a blender, combine the milk, egg substitute, oil, vanilla, and bananas just until combined. Add the bran cereal; process. Add the flour, sugar substitute, baking powder, baking soda, salt, and nutmeg. Process to combine, and scrape down the sides of the blender. Let the batter stand for 5 minutes. Stir gently.

2. Spray a griddle with cooking spray and preheat over medium-low heat. Pour the batter onto the hot griddle in the form of small pancakes. Cook until bubbles form on top and around the edges of the pancake. Flip the pancakes and cook until done on both sides. Top the pancakes with the vanilla butter.

Vanilla Butter

YIELD: 8 TABLESPOONS

This is a great topping to use on pancakes, waffles, or French toast instead of syrup for a hint of sweetness.

1/2 vanilla bean or 1 teaspoon vanilla
  extract
8 tablespoons (1 stick) unsalted butter,
  room temperature

1 teaspoon sugar substitute
1 teaspoon cinnamon

1. If using a vanilla bean, slice the bean lengthwise and scrape the seeds from inside the bean; discard the pod.

2. Combine the butter with the vanilla seeds or the extract, the sugar substitute, and the cinnamon. Mix well. Using a tablespoon, shape the butter into small servings and wrap the portions tightly in plastic wrap. Refrigerate.

Apple Crunch

YIELD: 6 SERVINGS

3/4 cup unsweetened apple juice
1/2 cup sugar substitute
1 tablespoon cornstarch
1 teaspoon grated lemon zest
2 (20-ounce) cans sliced apples, or 5
   apples, peeled, cored, and thinly sliced
Butter, for pan

CRUNCHY TOPPING:
1/4 cup all-purpose flour or low-fat
   biscuit mix
2 1/2 teaspoons sugar substitute
1 teaspoon ground cinnamon
1/2 teaspoon ground nutmeg
1/8 teaspoon ground allspice
4 tablespoons (1/2 stick) butter
1/4 cup quick-cooking oats
1/4 cup unsweetened flaked coconut

1. Preheat the oven to 400 degrees. In a medium saucepan, mix together the apple juice, sugar substitute, cornstarch, and lemon zest. Add the apples and turn the heat to high. Bring the apples to a boil, 3 to 5 minutes. Reduce the heat and simmer, uncovered, 5 to 7 minutes, until the juice is thickened and the apples soften. Set aside.

2. To prepare the crunchy topping: In a small bowl, combine the flour or biscuit mix, sugar substitute, cinnamon, nutmeg, and allspice. Cut in the butter with a pastry blender or a fork until the mixture resembles coarse crumbs. Stir in the oats and the coconut.

3. Lightly butter an 8-inch square baking pan. Spoon the apples into the pan. Sprinkle the crunchy topping over the apples. Bake until the topping is brown, about 25 minutes. Serve warm.

Diva-licious Chocolate Cake

YIELD: 10 SERVINGS

I LOVE chocolate, and this cake has a depth of flavor that comes from mixing the black coffee with high-quality cocoa powder. The combination of ingredients reduce the calories without sacrificing the rich flavors. Delicious!

Vegetable oil cooking spray
13/4 cups all-purpose flour
1/2 cup sugar substitute
1/2 cup brown sugar substitute
3/4 cup good-quality cocoa powder
11/2 teaspoons baking powder
11/2 teaspoons baking soda
1/2 teaspoon salt

11/4 cups low-fat buttermilk
1/4 cup vegetable oil
1/2 cup egg substitute
2 teaspoons vanilla extract
1 cup hot strong black coffee (instant works fine)
Fast and easy frosting (see following recipe) (optional)

1. Preheat the oven to 350 degrees. Grease a deep 9-inch cake pan or Bundt pan with cooking spray; set aside.

2. Blend the flour, white sugar substitute, brown sugar substitute, cocoa, baking powder, baking soda, and salt in large mixing bowl.

3. Combine the buttermilk, oil, egg substitute, vanilla, and coffee in a large bowl.

4. Add the flour mixture to the buttermilk mixture, blending with an electric mixer on medium speed. Mix the ingredients until smooth, but do not overbeat, about 2 minutes. Pour the batter into the pan.

5. Bake 35 minutes, until a toothpick inserted in the center of the cake comes out clean. Let the cake cool in the pan 5 minutes. Run a knife around the edges of the cake and invert the cake on to a plate. Cool and frost with fast and easy frosting, if desired.

Fast and Easy Frosting

YIELD: 12 SERVINGS

1 (1 1/2-ounce) package sugar-free instant
   pudding mix, any flavor
1 3/4 cups milk
1/4 teaspoon vanilla extract

1 (8-ounce) container light frozen
   whipped topping, thawed
1 (8-ounce) package low-fat cream cheese

1. In a medium bowl, combine the pudding mix, milk, and vanilla. Mix until smooth. Gently fold in whipped topping and cream cheese until completely blended. Spread over cake.

Pineapple Cream Pie

YIELD: 6 TO 8 SERVINGS

1 (20-ounce) can crushed pineapple,
   juice drained
1 (1-ounce) package sugar-free instant
   vanilla pudding mix (4-serving size)
1 cup low-fat sour cream

1 teaspoon sugar substitute
1 large banana, cut into thin rounds
1 teaspoon vanilla extract
1 (9-inch) graham cracker pie crust
1 (8-ounce) carton light whipped topping

1. Mix the pineapple, pudding mix, sour cream, sugar substitute, banana, and vanilla until well combined. Pour the filling into the graham cracker crust.

2. Spread the whipped topping on top of the pie to cover. Chill until set.

Cinnamon Bun Scones

YIELD: 10 SCONES

I love the taste of a cinnamon roll in a scone with the healthy addition of oats.

Vegetable oil cooking spray
2 cups self-rising flour or low-fat
  biscuit mix
1 cup quick oats or old-fashioned rolled
  oats
1/4 cup plus 2 tablespoons sugar substitute
8 tablespoons (1 stick) butter, chilled and
  cut into pieces

3/4 cup milk
1 egg, lightly beaten
1 teaspoon vanilla extract
1/2 cup pecans, toasted and chopped
2 teaspoons ground cinnamon

1. Preheat the oven to 425 degrees. Spray a cookie sheet with cooking spray. In a large bowl, combine the flour, oats, and 1/4 cup of the sugar substitute and mix well.

2. Cut in the butter with a pastry blender or 2 knives until the mixture resembles coarse crumbs.

3. In small bowl, combine the milk, egg, and vanilla; blend well. Add the egg mixture to the flour and butter all at once. Stir with fork or rubber spatula until the flour mixture is moistened.

4. In a small bowl, combine the remaining 2 tablespoons sugar substitute with the pecans and cinnamon; mix well. Sprinkle the pecan mixture evenly over the dough in the bowl. Gently stir the batter to swirl in the pecan mixture, but do not blend completely.

5. Drop the dough onto a nonstick cookie sheet by 1/4 cupfuls, placing the scones 2 inches apart.

6. Bake 11 to 13 minutes or until golden brown. Remove the scones to a wire rack and cool 5 minutes. Serve warm.

Getting Reacquainted

The New African-American Kitchen

Sometimes you need to take time and get reacquainted with yourself.

—Angela Shelf Medearis

When I first started producing The Kitchen Diva!, it seemed that the culinary mindset was that if you couldn't prepare something in thirty minutes or less, you shouldn't even try to cook! I call this style of break-neck meal preparation "beat the clock." All that's on the main course on this modern-day menu is a big helping of frustration with a side of stress.

If you're like me, you probably have a kitchen full of time-saving, labor-saving, space-saving, energy-saving appliances. We're constantly buying things that are guaranteed to get us in and out of the kitchen faster than ever before. What I want to know is, why am I still tired? It seems to me that we've taken all the time we've saved and have crammed it with even more activities. Sometimes we're too busy to cook at all. And the family dinner gathering is becoming a relic of the past.

From time to time, I clear my kitchen countertops of all the newfangled stuff and cook the old-fashioned way. I like to get out the recipes my mother and grandmother used. No zapping, no whirring, and no beeping. I've found that taking the time to chop up some onions by hand is relaxing. (If I need to sneak in a good stress-relieving crying jag, I can blame my tears on the onions.)

Putting on a big stewpot, filling it with good, fresh food, and stirring and smelling the contents for an hour or so is soothing. Kneading a mound of bread dough, punching it down, and watching it rise all release tension. And a slice of good-smelling bread, hot out of the oven and spread with butter, is like a mini-vacation for the senses.

From time to time, you need to meet with your family and friends around a dinner table loaded with home-cooked food. It's easier to forgive and forget when you're full. Every now and then, it's good to bake a cake or some cookies for someone you haven't had time to talk to in a while. Calling, e-mailing, or sending a card is faster, but there's just something about making a special dish for a friend that erases long absences.

My family has produced a long line of excellent cooks. My great-grandmother Angeline was a wonderful cook and trained my grandmother Willie Mae to be a culinary artist. Willie Mae passed down all she knew to my mother, Angeline. Unfortunately, my older sister, Sandra, and I weren't interested in learning to cook until after we had husbands and kitchens of our own. Why bother, when the most wonderful cook we both knew lived in our house? When I moved out, I remember calling my mother long distance several times a week to ask for detailed explanations about recipes I'd casually watched her prepare and enthusiastically eaten for years. My younger brother, Howard, and my baby sister, Marcia, were much wiser. They both learned to cook before leaving home.

Even though I was a lousy cook when I first got married, I really wanted to improve my culinary skills. After a number of disasters that my friends and family will never let me forget, I learned to "burn" with the best of them. The highest compliment an African-American Texan can give about your cooking is to tell you that "you really put your foot in that food!" When I heard that for the first time, I felt as if I had received the Oscar of African-American culinary awards.

I've passed down many of the recipes contained in this book to my daughter, Deanna. She was just like I was at her age. Why learn to cook when your momma loves cooking so much? She's finally developed an interest in cooking now that she's out on her own and has a child.

Anysa, my grandchild, has been in the kitchen cooking with me since she was two years old. In one of my favorite pictures of her, she's wearing Willie Mae's apron (wrapped around her tiny waist several times) helping out in the kitchen. Deanna and Anysa have both become good cooks and we spend almost every Sunday cooking, talking, and laughing in the kitchen.

The recipes in this section are ones I've especially enjoyed preparing for my family. Many were given to me by friends who love to cook, and others are my own delicious creations, featuring ingredients that weren't available to my mother or grandmother. These recipes reflect my attitude about life—none of them are overly complicated, and they're all infused with love for my family, friends, and history. Enjoy!

Appetizers, Soups, and Salads

Sesame-Cheese Spread

YIELD: 2 CUPS

The preparation of dishes containing sesame are direct contributions our African ancestors made to American cuisine.

2 cups shredded sharp cheddar cheese

2 (3-ounce) packages cream cheese, softened

1/4 cup toasted sesame seeds

1/4 cup milk

1 teaspoon soy sauce

1/2 teaspoon ground thyme

1/2 teaspoon salt

1. Mix all ingredients in a blender until smooth. Place in a serving bowl, cover, and refrigerate for at least 4 hours. Remove spread from refrigerator at least 1 hour before serving and let it stand at room temperature. Serve with crackers or toast.

Soul Food Dip

YIELD: 6 CUPS

This recipe has been a holiday hit in my family for years. It's simple, unique, and delicious.

1 tablespoon butter
1/2 medium onion, diced
1/2 cup diced celery
2 cloves garlic, minced
1 tablespoon olive oil
1 (10-ounce) package frozen chopped
    turnip greens, thawed
1/2 cup chopped fresh mushrooms

1/4 teaspoon grated lemon zest
1 (10 3/4-ounce) can low-sodium cream
    of mushroom soup, undiluted
1 (8-ounce) package cream cheese
1 teaspoon salt
1 teaspoon black pepper
1 teaspoon Worcestershire sauce
5 drops Tabasco sauce

1. In a large saucepan over medium-high heat, melt the butter. Sauté the onions, celery, and garlic until the onions are golden and the celery is tender, about 3 minutes.

2. Place the thawed, drained turnip greens in a clean kitchen towel or several sheets of food-safe paper towels and squeeze the greens to extract the water. In a blender or food processor, grind the turnip greens, mushrooms, and lemon zest together until smooth. Add the turnip greens mixture, soup, cream cheese, salt, pepper, Worcestershire sauce, and Tabasco sauce to the sautéed vegetables in the pan. Stirring occasionally, cook the mixture over medium heat until the ingredients are smooth and well combined, 7 to 10 minutes. Serve hot with crackers or pita chips.

Texas Caviar (Pickled Black-Eyed Peas)

YIELD: 6 SERVINGS

Because black-eyed peas are a contribution from Africa to America, this is a good dip to serve during a Kwanzaa celebration, and a great appetizer for New Year's Day.

2 (16-ounce) cans black-eyed peas
1/2 cup olive oil
1/4 cup red wine vinegar
1 clove garlic, smashed

1/4 cup chopped onion
1/4 cup chopped green bell pepper
1 teaspoon salt
1 teaspoon black pepper

1. Drain and rinse the peas; shake off the excess moisture, and put the peas in a small bowl. Add the remaining ingredients and mix thoroughly. Seal in an airtight container in the refrigerator. Refrigerate at least 2 days and up to 2 weeks before serving, stirring once a day to blend the flavors. Remove the garlic clove after 1 day. Serve with crackers.

Pickled Beets

YIELD: 6 SERVINGS

"Do a common thing, in an uncommon way." —Booker T. Washington

1/2 cup sugar
11/2 teaspoons mustard seed
1/4 teaspoon celery seed

11/2 teaspoons salt
1 cup apple cider vinegar
1 (16-ounce) jar sliced beets, drained

1. In a nonreactive saucepan, combine the sugar, mustard seed, celery seed, salt, and vinegar. Bring the mixture to a boil and pour it over the beets in a bowl, stirring gently until well coated. Let cool; cover. Refrigerate about 1 hour before serving.

Also pictured: Shrimp and Lobster Fajitas (page 235)

Easy Peanut Soup

YIELD: 10 SERVINGS

It's not what you call us, but what we answer to that matters. —Djuka proverb

2 tablespoons butter
2 tablespoons olive oil
1 medium onion, minced
1 cup sliced celery
2 tablespoons all-purpose flour
1/4 teaspoon cayenne pepper
1 teaspoon salt

4 (14 1/2-ounce) cans low-sodium
  chicken broth
1 cup smooth peanut butter
1 cup half-and-half
1/4 cup chopped salted peanuts, for
  garnish (optional)

1. Combine the butter and oil in a large pot over medium heat. Sauté the onions and celery until the onions have wilted and the celery is tender. Mix in the flour, cayenne, and salt, stirring until the ingredients are well blended. Slowly stir in the chicken broth. Stirring frequently, cook until the mixture comes to a boil, then immediately reduce heat to a simmer. Remove 1 cup of the broth; mix the 1 cup broth with the peanut butter and half-and-half in a small bowl. Stir the peanut butter mixture back into the remaining broth. Simmer 10 minutes, stirring frequently. Garnish with chopped peanuts, if desired.

Sweet Potato Soup

YIELD: 6 SERVINGS

"We wanted something for ourselves and for our children, so we took a chance with our lives." —Unita Blackwell

2 sweet potatoes, peeled and sliced
3 tablespoons butter
1 onion, minced
4 (14 1/2-ounce) cans low-sodium beef broth
3 tomatoes, finely chopped

1 teaspoon salt
1 teaspoon black pepper
1/2 teaspoon ground ginger
1 cup milk

1. In a large pot filled with water, boil the sweet potatoes until tender when pricked with a fork, 30 to 35 minutes. Discard the water. Peel the sweet potatoes and mash them with a potato masher or the back of a large spoon. Set them aside.

2. Melt the butter in the pot over medium heat. Add the onion and sauté until onion is soft. Add the beef broth, tomatoes, salt, pepper, and ginger. Cook until heated, about 5 minutes. Add the mashed potatoes and milk. Simmer over low heat for 5 minutes, stirring until smooth and free of lumps.

Hot Five-Bean Salad

YIELD: 10 SERVINGS

"It is the mind that makes the body." —Sojourner Truth

8 slices bacon

2/3 cup sugar

2 tablespoons cornstarch

1 1/2 teaspoons salt

1/8 teaspoon black pepper

3/4 cup white vinegar

1/2 cup water

1 (16-ounce) can kidney beans

1 (16-ounce) can cut green beans

1 (16-ounce) can lima beans

1 (16-ounce) can cut wax beans

1 (16-ounce) can garbanzo beans
   (chickpeas)

1. In a medium, nonreactive skillet over medium-high heat, cook the bacon until crisp. Remove the bacon from the pan and drain on paper towels. In the skillet, combine the sugar, cornstarch, salt, and pepper with the bacon drippings. Stir in the vinegar and water. Heat the mixture to boiling, stirring constantly. Drain all of the beans and add them to the skillet. Cover and simmer 15 to 20 minutes. Spoon the beans into a serving dish, crumble the bacon, and sprinkle it on top.

Crab Salad with Feta Cheese Dressing

YIELD: 4 SERVINGS

I love using imitation crabmeat in this recipe. Imitation crabmeat is made by using fish and parts of real crab to make a "paste" called surimi. Surimi means "minced fish," and the process was created in Japan more than 800 years ago and brought to the United States in 1975. Surimi is not that different from real crab, although it is lower in cholesterol. If you're on a budget, imitation crabmeat is a great substitute for the real thing, especially in this tasty recipe.

2 pounds cooked crabmeat, picked over
    for shells, or imitation crabmeat
1/2 pound feta cheese, finely crumbled
1/2 cup mayonnaise
1/2 cup buttermilk
2 tablespoons sour cream
2 stalks celery, chopped

3 tablespoons chopped scallion
1/2 tablespoon soy sauce
2 tablespoons white wine vinegar
1/4 teaspoon chopped garlic
1/2 teaspoon salt
1/2 teaspoon black pepper
Lettuce greens

1. Mix all the ingredients except the lettuce together by hand. Serve on a bed of lettuce.

Main Dishes

Quick and Zesty Black Beans with Rice

YIELD: 4 SERVINGS

No meat? No matter; serve this recipe over brown rice and you won't even miss the meat! This is one of my husband Michael's favorite vegetarian dishes.

2 teaspoons vegetable or olive oil
1/2 cup chopped onion
1/2 cup chopped red or green bell pepper
1/2 cup diced fresh mild chile peppers,
    such as Anaheim
1 tomato, chopped
1 clove garlic, minced

1 teaspoon dried oregano
2 (16-ounce) cans black beans, drained
    and rinsed
1/4 teaspoon sugar
1 teaspoon salt
1 teaspoon black pepper
2 cups hot cooked brown rice

1. In a saucepan over moderate heat, heat the oil until hot but not smoking. Add the onion, bell pepper, chile peppers, tomato, garlic, and oregano. Cook until the vegetables wilt, stirring occasionally, 5 to 8 minutes. Add the beans, sugar, salt, and pepper. Cover, reduce the heat to low, and simmer 15 minutes, stirring occasionally. Serve on a bed of rice.

MICROWAVE VARIATION:
Put the oil, vegetables, and seasonings in a microwave dish. Cook on high 7 minutes, or until the vegetables wilt. Stir in the beans, cover, and cook on medium 10 minutes.

Chicken-Fried Steak with Brown Gravy

YIELD: 6 SERVINGS

This dish is a family (and Texas) favorite. Bring on the mashed potatoes!

2 pounds round steak, cut into 6 serving
   pieces
1¹/2 teaspoons salt
1¹/2 teaspoons black pepper
1¹/2 teaspoons garlic powder
2 cups all-purpose flour

¹/2 teaspoon cayenne pepper
1 egg
1¹/2 cups water
2 cups vegetable oil
1¹/2 teaspoons steak sauce
1¹/2 cups warm water

1. Season the steak pieces with ¹/2 teaspoon each of the salt, black pepper, and garlic powder. Season the flour with ¹/2 teaspoon each of the salt, black pepper, garlic powder, and cayenne pepper. Stir with a fork to blend the ingredients.

2. In a medium bowl, combine the egg, the water, and the remaining ¹/2 teaspoon each of the salt, black pepper, and garlic powder. Coat the steak pieces in the seasoned flour, shaking off the excess flour. Then dip the steak pieces in the egg-and-water mixture. Shake off the excess egg mixture and dip the steak pieces back into the flour. Shake off the excess flour and set the steak aside on a sheet pan. Repeat until all the pieces are coated. Reserve 3 tablespoons of the remaining flour. If possible, refrigerate the steak for at least 30 minutes to allow the coating to adhere.

3. In a large skillet, heat the oil over high heat until a pinch of flour sizzles when sprinkled on top. Place the steak pieces in the oil. Do not crowd the meat in the pan. Brown the pieces on both sides until done, 5 to 7 minutes on each side. Remove to a paper towel–covered plate and set aside in a warm place.

4. Pour off all the oil from the skillet except about 3 tablespoons, leaving as many of the brown bits from frying the steak as possible. Stir 3 tablespoons of the reserved seasoned flour into the oil. Cook over moderate heat, stirring, until the flour is lightly browned, being careful not to burn it. Stir in the steak sauce. Slowly add the warm water to the flour mixture, about ¹/4 cup at a time, stirring until the gravy is smooth and thin. Bring the gravy to a boil to thicken, adding more water, if necessary. Simmer the gravy over low heat, 2 to 3 minutes. Put the steaks on serving plates with a spoonful of gravy in the center of each.

Meat Loaf with Tomato Sauce Gravy

YIELD: 4 SERVINGS

I don't know what it is about men and meat loaf. I even had an employee request that I make him one for a Christmas present! I asked a friend what the big deal was about meat loaf and he said, "It's meat in a loaf and you don't have to chew it very much. What's not to like?"

1 egg
1 pound lean ground beef
1 pound lean pork sausage
1/4 cup prepared salsa
1/2 tablespoon steak sauce
1 teaspoon salt
1 teaspoon black pepper
1 small onion, minced
1 clove garlic, minced
1 green bell pepper, seeded and minced
1/2 cup dry bread crumbs

TOMATO SAUCE GRAVY:
1 onion, diced
2 stalks celery, diced
2 tablespoons butter
1 (16-ounce) can whole tomatoes, chopped, with liquid
1/2 teaspoon Worcestershire sauce
1/4 teaspoon Tabasco sauce

1. Preheat the oven to 350 degrees. In a large bowl, beat the egg lightly. Add the ground beef, sausage, salsa, steak sauce, salt, and black pepper and mix well, using your hands. Add the onion, garlic, bell pepper, and bread crumbs and gently mix until well blended, but do not overwork the mixture as it will make the meatloaf tough. Turn the meat mixture into a baking pan and pat into a rounded mound. Cover with foil and bake 30 minutes.

2. To prepare the tomato gravy: On the stovetop or in a bowl in the microwave on medium power for 3 minutes, sauté the onion and celery in the butter until tender. Stir in the tomatoes and their liquid and the Worcestershire and Tabasco sauces. Simmer, uncovered, stirring occasionally, 10 minutes, if using the stovetop preparation or for an additional 3 to 5 minutes, on medium power, stirring after 2 minutes, if using a microwave.

3. Remove the meat loaf from the oven and drain the fat from the baking pan. Pour the tomato gravy over the meat loaf, letting it run down the sides. Return the meat loaf to the oven. Do not cover it. Bake 30 minutes, or until done.

Barbecued Short Ribs of Beef

YIELD: 4 TO 6 SERVINGS

> "No race can prosper till it learns that there is as much dignity in tilling a field as in writing a poem." —Booker T. Washington

3 to 4 pounds short ribs of beef
1 cup all-purpose flour, for dredging
1 teaspoon salt
1 teaspoon black pepper
1 teaspoon dried sage
1 teaspoon dried thyme
1/2 teaspoon cayenne pepper
1/4 cup vegetable oil

1 (16-ounce) can chunk pineapple with juice
1/2 cup water
2 cups ketchup or barbecue sauce
3 tablespoons Worcestershire sauce
3 medium onions, chopped
2 cloves garlic, minced
1/2 teaspoon dry mustard
1/2 cup packed brown sugar

1. Preheat the oven to 300 degrees. Season the beef and the flour with equal portions of the salt, pepper, sage, thyme, and cayenne pepper. Dredge the pieces in the seasoned flour, and put the ribs in a 2-quart casserole. Drizzle with oil, cover, and bake for 20 minutes.

2. In a saucepan, combine the remaining ingredients and simmer 5 minutes. Pour over the ribs. Cover and bake 2 to 3 hours, or until the meat is fork-tender, turning and basting with the sauce every 30 minutes. Remove the cover 30 minutes before the beef is done to permit browning. When done, remove the meat from the casserole and skim the fat from the sauce. Serve with the sauce on the side.

Chicken with Rosemary and Orange Sauce

YIELD: 6 SERVINGS

"Eating when you are hungry and sleeping when you are sleepy. That is the ultimate wisdom." —Bessie Copage

6 boneless, skinless chicken breast halves
1 teaspoon salt
1 teaspoon black pepper
3/4 teaspoon dried rosemary, crushed
between your fingers

1 1/2 tablespoons vegetable oil
1 cup orange juice
1 teaspoon grated orange zest

1. Season the chicken with the salt, pepper, and rosemary. In a skillet over moderate heat, heat the oil until hot but not smoking and brown the chicken on both sides. Remove the chicken to a plate; pour off the fat in the skillet and discard.

2. In the skillet, combine the orange juice and zest and simmer for 5 minutes, stirring occasionally. Add the chicken, cover, and simmer, stirring occasionally, for 20 minutes, or until the chicken is done and the sauce has thickened.

Crispy Baked Fish

YIELD: 4 SERVINGS

This simple recipe for baked Parmesan-coated fish guarantees that [...] kitchen in record time yet still make a wonderful meal.

1½ pounds white fish fillets (trout, perch, catfish, or tilapia)
¼ cup olive oil
1 teaspoon salt
1 teaspoon black pepper

1 teaspoon poultry seasoning
1 clove garlic, minced
Vegetable oil cooking spray
1 cup grated Parmesan cheese
¾ cup seasoned bread crumbs

1. Wash the fillets under cold running water, pat dry with paper towels, and cut into serving pieces. In a small bowl, combine the oil, salt, black pepper, poultry seasoning, and garlic. Arrange the fish fillets in a large flat dish. Pour the oil mixture over the fillets. Let the fish sit 10 minutes, then turn the pieces.

2. Preheat the oven to 400 degrees. Spray a cookie sheet or baking dish with cooking spray. Place the pan in the oven to preheat for crispier fish.

3. Put the Parmesan cheese and bread crumbs on separate sheets of waxed paper or on separate plates. Coat each piece of fish with the cheese, then dredge in the bread crumbs. Arrange the fish on the cookie sheet or in the baking dish. Bake 8 to 10 minutes. Turn the pieces over and bake an additional 5 to 7 minutes, until the coating is crisp and golden.

Also pictured: Mess of Greens (page 243) and Cornbread (page 156)

Chicken Stuffed with Spinach and Artichokes

YIELD: 4 TO 6 SERVINGS

I'm always thinking about ways to use simple ingredients to jazz up roasted chicken, a company favorite. I created this dish for my daughter Deanna, because she loves artichokes and spinach. It has become a family favorite.

1 (8-ounce) package cream cheese, softened
1/4 cup mayonnaise
1/4 cup grated Parmesan cheese
1/4 cup grated Romano cheese
1/4 cup shredded mozzarella cheese
2 teaspoons salt
2 teaspoons poultry seasoning
1 teaspoon black pepper
1/8 teaspoon nutmeg

1 (14-ounce) can artichoke hearts, drained and chopped
1 (10-ounce) package frozen, chopped spinach, thawed and drained
1/2 cup bread crumbs
1 (3 1/2-pound) fryer chicken
1/4 cup olive oil
1 clove garlic, minced
1 teaspoon onion powder

1. Preheat the oven to 400 degrees. In a medium bowl, mix together the cream cheese, mayonnaise, Parmesan cheese, Romano cheese, mozzarella cheese, and 1 teaspoon each of the salt and poultry seasoning and 1/2 teaspoon of the black pepper; add the nutmeg. Gently stir in artichoke hearts, spinach, and bread crumbs.

2. Wash the chicken, butterfly it, and remove any interior pieces of fat; pat dry thoroughly with paper towels. Rub the oil on the skin of the chicken and flip it over and rub it on the inside of the chicken.

3. Season the chicken on both sides with the remaining 1 teaspoon each salt and poultry seasoning, the remaining 1/2 teaspoon black pepper, the garlic, and the onion powder.

4. Loosen the skin of the chicken by gently pushing your finger between the meat and the skin to make space for the stuffing. Stuff the spinach mixture under the chicken skin, pressing downward gently and pushing it from the breast to the thigh and leg meat. Leftover stuffing can be placed in a small casserole dish.

5. Place the chicken on a rack in a shallow baking pan, cover it loosely with a sheet of aluminum foil, and place it in the oven. Bake the additional stuffing until it is hot and bubbling, 15 to 20 minutes. Bake the chicken 30 to 40 minutes. Remove the foil and continue to roast until the skin is crispy and brown and the internal temperature reads 165 degrees on an instant-read thermometer, about 30 minutes. The temperature should be taken in 2 parts of the bird: the innermost part of the thigh, and at the thickest part of the breast with the thermometer without touching the bone.

Shrimp and Lobster Fajitas

YIELD: 6 TO 8 SERVINGS

"I don't believe in failure. It's not failure if you enjoyed the process." —Oprah Winfrey

1 tablespoon sweet paprika

1 tablespoon salt

1 tablespoon garlic powder

1 tablespoon onion powder

3/4 teaspoon black pepper

1/2 teaspoon Tabasco sauce

1/2 teaspoon dried thyme

1/2 teaspoon dried oregano

2 pounds medium or large shrimp, shelled and deveined

1 pound lobster meat, cut into 1-inch chunks

1 onion, quartered and cut into large strips

1 green bell pepper, seeded and cut into large strips

1/2 cup olive oil

1/2 cup fresh lime juice

16 flour tortillas

Salsa (optional)

Guacamole (optional)

Refried beans (optional)

1. In a small bowl, blend the paprika, salt, garlic powder, onion powder, black pepper, Tabasco sauce, thyme, and oregano. Combine half the spice mixture with the shrimp and the other half with the lobster.

2. In a large skillet over moderate heat, sauté the onion and bell pepper in the olive oil, 2 minutes. Add the lobster and cook 2 minutes, then add the shrimp and cook 2 minutes. Add the lime juice and cook until shellfish are heated through. Serve in flour tortillas with salsa, guacamole, and refried beans, or serve over rice or pasta.

Sunday Dinner Pork Chops

YIELD: 8 SERVINGS

"You worry too much about what goes into your mouth, and not enough about what comes out of it." —Leah Chase

8 (1/2-inch-thick) pork chops
1 teaspoon olive oil
1/2 teaspoon white vinegar
1 teaspoon salt
1 teaspoon black pepper
1 teaspoon poultry seasoning
2 tablespoons vegetable oil
1 (28-ounce) can whole tomatoes, with liquid
1 cup finely chopped onion
2 bay leaves
4 black peppercorns
1 tablespoon sugar
2 cloves garlic, minced
1 teaspoon dried oregano
1/4 teaspoon nutmeg
1 (16-ounce) can string beans
1 (16-ounce) can whole-kernel corn

1. Trim all the fat from the pork chops, rinse, and dry with paper towels. Combine the olive oil and vinegar and coat the pork chops with the mixture. Season the pork chops with the salt, black pepper, and poultry seasoning.

2. In a deep skillet over medium heat, heat the vegetable oil until hot but not smoking; brown the chops lightly on both sides. Remove the pork chops from the pan and set aside.

3. Add the tomatoes, onion, bay leaves, peppercorns, sugar, garlic, oregano, and nutmeg to the skillet. Bring the ingredients to a boil over medium heat. Return the pork chops to the skillet, cover, and reduce the heat to low. Simmer 15 minutes. Uncover and remove the bay leaves. Return the heat to medium and cook 10 minutes, stirring occasionally. Drain the string beans and corn and stir them in. Simmer 10 minutes. Serve hot.

Spareribs Stuffed with Wild-Rice Dressing

YIELD: 6 SERVINGS

I love this dish because it's so simple and looks so elegant. It's a guaranteed crowd-pleaser.

2 (2- to 3-pound) whole slabs pork
    spareribs, about the same length
1 1/2 teaspoons salt, or to taste
1 teaspoon black pepper, plus more to taste
1/2 cup all-purpose flour
1 teaspoon dried sage
1 teaspoon dried thyme
3 cups cooked and cooled wild or
    brown rice

1 onion, sliced
2 cloves garlic, minced
1 green bell pepper, seeded and diced
2 stalks celery, including tops, diced
1/2 cup boiling water
1 cup cream of mushroom sauce
    (see following recipe)
2 tablespoons steak sauce

1. Preheat the oven to 400 degrees. Trim the fat from the pork slabs and season with salt and pepper to taste. Combine the flour, sage, 1 teaspoon black pepper, and the thyme. Dredge the slabs in the seasoned flour until they are lightly coated.

2. Lay 1 slab so that the ends turn up in a roasting pan with a tight-fitting lid. In a small bowl, combine the rice, onion, garlic, bell pepper, and celery. Spread the mixture on the ribs.

3. In a small bowl, stir together the boiling water, the cream of mushroom sauce, and the steak sauce until smooth. Pour half of the mixture over the ribs.

4. Place the second slab of ribs on top of the rice mixture so that the ends turn down. Fasten the slabs together with skewers. Pour the remaining half of the mixture over the ribs. Cover the pan tightly and bake, basting frequently, until the ribs are brown and tender, 40 to 60 minutes.

Cream of Mushroom Sauce

YIELD: 1 CUP

1 tablespoon butter
3 tablespoons all-purpose flour
1 teaspoon salt
1 teaspoon black pepper

1/2 cup broth (beef, chicken, or vegetable)
1/2 cup milk
1/4 cup chopped mushrooms

1. Melt the butter in a saucepan over medium-low heat. Stir in the flour 1 tablespoon at a time until the mixture is smooth, then remove the pan from the heat. Stir in the salt and pepper.

2. Slowly whisk in the broth and the milk, a little at a time, stirring to keep mixture smooth. Stir in the mushrooms. Return to the pan to the heat and bring the sauce to a gentle boil to thicken, stirring constantly.

Pecan Fish

YIELD: 4 SERVINGS

"I could draw a circle on a piece of paper and my mother made me feel like van Gogh." —Damon Wayans

2 tablespoons milk
3 tablespoons Dijon mustard

4 (1/2-pound) catfish fillets
1 cup ground pecans

1. Preheat the oven to 500 degrees. In a small bowl, combine the milk and mustard. Dip the fillets into the mustard mixture. Coat the fillets with the pecans, shaking off the excess. Put the fillets on a greased baking sheet and bake 8 to 10 minutes.

Marcia's Passionate Pasta

YIELD: 6 SERVINGS

My romantic younger sister dreamed up this combination for a Valentine's Day dinner. It's a wonderful way to celebrate a special day.

6 Italian sausages: 3 mild, 3 spicy, 1 1/2
   pounds total
2 tablespoons olive oil
2 cloves garlic, minced
1 onion, finely chopped
1 green bell pepper, seeded and diced
1/2 pound medium shrimp, shelled and
   deveined
1 cup sliced mushrooms

3 plum tomatoes, sliced
1 teaspoon Italian seasoning
1 teaspoon sugar
1 teaspoon salt
1 teaspoon black pepper
1 teaspoon dried basil
1/4 teaspoon cayenne pepper
1 (8-ounce) can tomato sauce
1 1/2 pounds fettuccine, cooked

1. Remove the sausage meat from the casings. Roll the meat into meatballs. In a large skillet over moderate heat, heat the olive oil until hot but not smoking. Fry the meatballs in the olive oil until they are browned on all sides. Remove from the skillet and drain on paper towels.

2. Add the garlic, onion, and bell pepper to the skillet and sauté until the onion is golden brown. Add the shrimp, mushrooms, tomatoes, and seasonings and sauté, 5 to 8 minutes. Add the tomato sauce and sausage balls and simmer the sauce over low heat, 30 minutes, stirring occasionally. Serve over the hot fettuccine.

Vegetables and Side Dishes

Sweet-and-Sour Cabbage

YIELD: 6 SERVINGS

"I had...found that motherhood was a profession by itself just like schoolteaching and lecturing." —Ida B. Wells-Barnett

1 head cabbage, cored and shredded
1/4 cup water
2 teaspoons salt
1 tablespoon sugar

1 teaspoon black pepper
1 tablespoon all-purpose flour
2 tablespoons white vinegar
1 tablespoon butter

1. Put the cabbage, water, and 1 teaspoon of the salt in a medium saucepan. Cover and simmer over medium heat, 10 minutes. Add the sugar, the remaining 1 teaspoon salt, the black pepper, flour, vinegar, and butter; mix well. Cook until the cabbage is tender, 5 to 10 minutes.

Oven-Roasted Potatoes

YIELD: 4 SERVINGS

"If you are not feeling good about you, what you're wearing on the outside doesn't mean a thing." —Leontyne Price

Vegetable oil cooking spray
1/2 cup olive oil
1 tablespoon dried rosemary, crumbled
1 tablespoon dried thyme, crumbled
1 tablespoon dried oregano, crumbled
4 cloves garlic, minced

2 teaspoons salt
1 teaspoon black pepper
4 medium potatoes, cut into 1/2-inch slices
    or wedges
1 medium red bell pepper, seeded and cut
    into 1-inch squares

1. Preheat the oven to 475 degrees. Spray a shallow baking pan or a baking sheet with sides with cooking spray and preheat the pan in the oven for crisper potatoes.

2. Combine the remaining ingredients except the potatoes and bell pepper in the prepared pan. Add the potatoes and bell pepper and toss to coat. Arrange in a single layer. Bake 30 to 35 minutes, tossing 2 to 3 times during baking, until the potatoes are tender and lightly browned.

Kale with Tomato and Onion

YIELD: 8 SERVINGS

1½ pounds fresh kale, washed, stems and yellow leaves removed, and torn into small pieces

2 teaspoons vegetable oil

1 cup chopped tomato

3/4 cup chopped onion

2 teaspoons fresh lemon juice

1 clove garlic, minced

1 teaspoon salt

1 teaspoon black pepper

1. Put the wet, freshly washed kale in a large Dutch oven. Cook, uncovered, over medium heat, stirring occasionally, 20 to 30 minutes, until wilted and tender. No added water is needed, as the greens will give off their own liquid.

2. In a large skillet, heat the oil over medium heat until hot but not smoking. Add the tomato and onion and cook, stirring constantly, until the vegetables are tender, 5 to 8 minutes. Add the cooked kale, lemon juice, garlic, salt, and pepper. Cook 4 to 5 minutes, stirring constantly.

Greens

When my parents moved into a new home, my mother transported her beloved turnip, collard, and mustard greens in squat wooden tubs. She moved her garden along with the rest of the household goods as if it were the most natural thing in the world. She had to have something to nurture and love, a piece of ground to tend, until a new garden could be planted.

After my visits, my mother usually gives me a brown paper sack full of greens fresh from her garden. I enjoy eating greens, but I hate to clean them—you have to examine each leaf like a skeptic checking out a used car. Greens must be soaked in a cool salt bath and rinsed several times, or eating them is like eating a mouthful of sand. However, I gladly clean vast quantities of turnip, collard, and mustard greens just for the privilege of watching my mother care for her garden.

My mother's garden is a kind of poetry. The lines of corn and tomato plants are all neatly rhythmical. The broccoli, tomatoes, collards, mustard greens, onions, and bell pepper plants each have a definitive marker. The rich, warm black earth gives off a wonderful smell.

I like to sit between the rows while my mother picks the greens for me to take home. She always refuses my offers of help, because she knows that both of my thumbs are black in more ways than one. I still can't tell a budding green plant from a healthy weed.

I enjoy listening to her tell me why the bugs are so bad this year, or why this or that has gone to seed so early in the season. I pretend to understand and offer polite words of sympathy in the proper places. Her voice drifts over the rows to me as I half-close my eyes and enjoy the sun. The rays warm the top of my head and the heat flows through my body. I relax as completely as if I'm having a hot bubble bath.

My mother works quickly, her hands almost a blur before my half-shut eyes. The hot sun makes me drowsy. When the sack is full, she presents her offering to me with a big smile. "Ann," she says, "these are really going to be good."

I could have anything I want from my mother's garden, vegetables that I love to eat, that require little preparation. Plump, ripe tomatoes; good, firm broccoli; and ears of sweet corn are mine for the asking. But I know that my mother wants me to have what she loves and enjoys the most: the greens.

Mess of Greens

YIELD: 8 SERVINGS

> Greens include any vegetable in the cabbage family that doesn't form a compact head, such as collards, mustards, turnips, spinach, and kale. If the stems are tough, don't throw them away. There are nutrients in the stems, so save them, chop them up into small pieces and freeze them. You can add the stems to soups and stews, sauté them when you sauté your onions, or add them in just the way you add in carrots.

4 pounds greens (mixture of kale, collards, mustard, turnips, or spinach)
1/4 cup olive oil
1 large onion, sliced
1 tablespoon salt
6 cloves garlic, diced

1 jalapeño, diced
1 tablespoon sugar
1 tablespoon black pepper
5 cups water
6 sun-dried tomatoes in oil, sliced (optional)

1. Remove any brown spots or blemishes from the greens, and wash the greens in cold water 3 or 4 times to ensure that they are clean and free of insects. Roll the cleaned greens up and slice them into smaller pieces so they'll cook evenly. Remove and reserve any large stems.

2. Heat the olive oil in a large pot over low heat. Place the onions in the pot, season them with 1/2 tablespoon salt, and sweat them, 10 to 12 minutes, stirring occasionally. Add the garlic, jalapeño, sugar, remaining 1/2 tablespoon salt, and the black pepper to the pot and sauté the mixture about 5 minutes. Add the greens and the water to the pot and continue cooking over medium-low heat, 45 minutes to 1 hour, stirring once after 30 to 40 minutes.

3. Test the greens for tenderness by piercing the stems with a fork or knife. Cook the greens another 10 to 15 minutes, if needed. Place the greens in a bowl with the pot "likker." Pour 2 tablespoons of the sun-dried tomato oil over the greens and sprinkle with the chopped sun-dried tomatoes. Serve the greens with the traditional Southern condiments: vinegar, hot sauce, hot peppers in vinegar, or wine vinegar, and chopped onions, if desired.

Rice Primavera

YIELD: 8 SERVINGS

"Make some muscle in your head, but use the muscle in your heart."
—Imanu Amiri Baraka

1 clove garlic, peeled and left whole

2 teaspoons olive oil

2 cups broccoli florets

1 cup sliced zucchini

1 cup sliced mushrooms

1 teaspoon salt

1 teaspoon black pepper

1/2 teaspoon sugar

1 medium tomato, seeded and chopped

1/4 cup chopped parsley

1/3 cup reduced-calorie mayonnaise

1/2 cup skim milk

1/4 cup freshly grated Parmesan cheese

1/4 teaspoon ground white pepper

3 cups cooked rice

1. In a large skillet over moderate heat, cook the garlic clove in the olive oil about 3 minutes. Discard the garlic. Add the broccoli, zucchini, mushrooms, salt, black pepper, and sugar to the skillet and cook until crisp-tender, 5 to 10 minutes. Add the tomato and parsley, and cook 1 minute longer. Remove the vegetables and set aside.

2. Add to the skillet the mayonnaise, milk, cheese, and white pepper and cook over moderate heat, stirring, until smooth. Add the rice; toss to coat. Remove the skillet from the heat and stir in the vegetables.

Rolls and Desserts

Five-Flavor Pound Cake

YIELD: 1 (12-CUP) BUNDT CAKE

I love the way this cake looks, the way it fills the room with its wonderful aroma, and the way it tastes!

1 cup (2 sticks) softened butter, plus more
   for pan
1/2 cup vegetable shortening
1/3 cup vegetable oil
3 cups sugar
5 eggs, lightly beaten
3 cups all-purpose flour, plus more for pan
1 teaspoon baking powder

1 teaspoon salt
1 cup milk
1 teaspoon vanilla extract
1 teaspoon butter flavoring
1 teaspoon rum flavoring
1 teaspoon coconut extract
1 teaspoon lemon extract

1. Preheat the oven to 325 degrees. In a large bowl, combine the butter, shortening, and oil. Add the sugar and beat well. Add the eggs and combine well. Add 1 cup of the flour, the baking powder, salt, and 1/3 cup of the milk and mix. Add 1 more cup flour and mix. Add 1/3 cup milk and mix. Add 1/2 cup flour and mix. Add the last 1/3 cup milk and mix. Add the last 1/2 cup of the flour and mix. Add all the flavorings and mix well.

2. Lightly grease a 12-cup Bundt pan and dust with flour. Pour the batter into the pan. Bake until a toothpick inserted in the center of the cake comes out clean, about 1 hour and 20 minutes. Remove the cake from the oven and let cool about 1 hour. Slide a knife around the edges of the cake pan and invert the cake onto a plate.

Dinner Rolls

YIELD: 3 DOZEN ROLLS

A friend fixed two dozen of these rolls for me to serve with our Thanksgiving dinner. I sampled one before freezing them, then another, and another. I had to get the recipe from her so I could fix another batch.

2 packages active dry yeast (rapid-rising is best)
7 cups all-purpose flour
2¹/2 cups milk
¹/2 cup sugar

¹/2 cup vegetable shortening
2 teaspoons salt
2 eggs
8 tablespoons (1 stick) butter, plus more for greasing the bowl

1. In a large bowl, sift together the yeast and 3¹/2 cups flour.

2. In a saucepan over medium heat, combine the milk, sugar, shortening, and salt. Heat but do not boil.

3. Add the liquid gradually to the yeast and flour mixture. Beat the eggs and add to the mixture. Slowly add the remaining flour. Knead or mix until smooth and elastic, about 10 minutes.

4. Lightly grease a large bowl with butter. Form the dough into a ball, set in the bowl, cover, and leave in a warm, draft-free area. Let the dough rise for 10 minutes (if using rapid-rising yeast) or until it has doubled in size. Punch the dough down and roll out on a floured surface, about ¹/2 inch thick. With a 3-inch biscuit cutter, cut out circles.

5. Melt the butter and brush onto the dough circles. Fold the circles in half and place close together in 9-inch cake pans, 1 dozen rolls to a pan. Let the rolls rise in a warm place until doubled in size, about 1¹/2 to 2 hours. They need not be covered.

6. Preheat the oven to 400 degrees. Bake the rolls until brown, 15 to 20 minutes. Brush the hot rolls with more melted butter, if desired.

Toasted Butter Pecan Cake

YIELD: 1 FILLED AND FROSTED (9-INCH) LAYER CAKE

"I am because we are: and since we are, therefore I am." —John Mbuti

11 tablespoons butter, plus more for pans
2 cups sifted all-purpose flour, plus more
  for pans
1 1/3 cups coarsely chopped pecans
1 1/3 cups sugar
3 eggs
1 1/4 teaspoons vanilla extract
1 1/4 teaspoons baking powder
1/4 teaspoon salt
2/3 cup milk

BUTTER PECAN FROSTING:
4 tablespoons (1/2 stick) butter, softened
1 pound confectioners' sugar, sifted
1 teaspoon vanilla extract
4 to 6 tablespoons heavy cream
1/3 cup toasted pecans

1. Preheat the oven to 350 degrees. Grease 2 (9-inch) cake pans and dust with flour. Put the pecans on a baking sheet and toast 5 to 8 minutes, stirring frequently. Watch carefully so they don't burn. Let the pecans cool. Set aside 1/3 cup toasted pecans for the frosting.

2. To prepare the cake, cream the butter, then gradually add the sugar, beating until fluffy. Add the eggs one at a time, beating well after each addition; blend in the vanilla extract. Sift together the flour, baking powder, and salt; add to the creamed mixture alternating with the milk. Stir in 1 cup toasted pecans. Turn the batter into the prepared pans. Bake 25 to 30 minutes, or until a knife inserted in the center comes out clean; cool thoroughly.

3. To prepare the frosting: Cream the butter; gradually add the sugar, beating well until fluffy. Stir in the vanilla extract. Add cream until the mixture reaches spreading consistency. Stir in the reserved 1/3 cup pecans.

4. Fill and frost the cake with the butter pecan frosting.

Easy Fudge Pecan Pie

YIELD: 2 (9-INCH) PIES

"Every man got a right to his own mistakes. Ain't no man that ain't made any."
—Joe Louis

3 1/2 cups milk

3/4 cup unsweetened cocoa powder

4 cups sugar

1 cup all-purpose flour

1 tablespoon vanilla extract

8 tablespoons (1 stick) butter, softened

1/2 teaspoon salt

2 cups pecans

2 unbaked 9-inch pie shells (page TK)

Chopped pecans (optional)

Coconut flakes (optional)

1. Preheat the oven to 375 degrees. In a medium saucepan, mix the milk and cocoa and bring to a fast simmer. Remove from the heat.

2. In another bowl, combine the sugar, flour, vanilla, butter, salt, and pecans. Pour the milk and cocoa mixture over the sugar and pecan mixture. Mix well. Pour the mixture into 2 unbaked pie shells. Sprinkle with chopped pecans and/or coconut, if desired. Bake for 40 to 45 minutes, or until set.

Quick and Easy Pie Crusts

YIELD: PASTRY FOR 1 DOUBLE-CRUST (9-INCH) PIE

This is my favorite pie crust recipe. Be sure that you measure the flour exactly as it makes a difference in the texture of the crust.

3 cups all-purpose flour

1 teaspoon salt

1 1/2 cups butter-flavored shortening

1/4 cup plus 1 tablespoon water

1 tablespoon white vinegar

1 egg

1. In the bowl of a food processor, blend the flour and salt. Add in the shortening and pulse to combine. In a small bowl, combine the water, vinegar, and egg. Slowly add the water mixture to the flour mixture in the food processor and mix well. Follow rolling and baking instructions for Pie Crust (page 250).

Note: For desserts, add 1 teaspoon sugar to the dough. This dough can be frozen. To freeze, roll in a ball and wrap well in waxed paper. When ready to use, thaw completely before rolling out.

Walnut Sweet Potato Pie

YIELD: 1 (9-INCH) PIE

"There's no need to hurry, yet no time to lose." —Bessie Copage

2 medium sweet potatoes, baked until
    tender then peeled, still warm
4 tablespoons (1/2 stick) butter
1 (14-ounce) can sweetened condensed
    milk
1 teaspoon grated orange zest
1 teaspoon vanilla extract
1 teaspoon ground cinnamon
1/2 teaspoon ground nutmeg
1/4 teaspoon salt

2 eggs
1 unbaked 9-inch pie shell (page 250)

WALNUT TOPPING:
1 egg
3 tablespoons dark corn syrup
3 tablespoons packed light brown sugar
1 tablespoon butter, melted
1/2 teaspoon maple flavoring
1 cup chopped walnuts

1. Preheat the oven to 350 degrees. In a large bowl, mash the hot sweet potatoes with the butter until smooth. Add the condensed milk, orange zest, vanilla extract, cinnamon, nutmeg, salt, and eggs and beat until the mixture is creamy. Pour into the pie shell. Bake 30 minutes.

2. Meanwhile, prepare the topping: In a small bowl, combine the egg, corn syrup, brown sugar, butter, and maple flavoring. Stir in the walnuts.

3. Remove the pie from the oven; spoon the topping evenly over the top. Bake 20 to 25 minutes longer, or until the pie is firm and golden brown. Serve warm or chilled. Refrigerate any leftovers.

Pie Crust

YIELD: PASTRY FOR 1 SINGLE-CRUST (9-INCH) PIE

"No matter what accomplishment you make, somebody helps you." —Althea Gibson

1/2 cup vegetable shortening
2 teaspoons confectioners' sugar
1 teaspoon salt

1 1/4 cups all-purpose flour, plus more
   for dusting
1 cup cake flour
4 to 5 tablespoons ice water

1. Cream together the shortening, sugar, and salt. Combine the all-purpose and cake flours and sift over the shortening mixture. Cut the shortening into the flour until crumbly. Sprinkle ice water over the mixture and stir just to moisten. Gather up the mixture with your fingers and form into a smooth, not sticky, ball of dough. Do not overmix the dough.

2. On a lightly floured surface, roll the dough 1/8-inch thick. Transfer to a 9-inch pie pan. Trim the edges to 1/2 inch beyond the edge of the pan. Fold the edges under and flute by pinching the edges between your thumb and finger. Fill the crust with desired filling and bake according to the directions in the recipe, or bake "blind" as follows: Place another pie pan inside the crust to prevent shrinking or bubbling. Bake at 350 degrees until light brown, 20 to 25 minutes.

Lemon Icebox Pie

YIELD: 1 (9-INCH) PIE

"Before you marry, keep both eyes open; after marriage, shut one." —Jamaican proverb

CRUST:
1 1/2 cups graham cracker crumbs
1 teaspoon sugar
4 tablespoons (1/2 stick) butter, melted

FILLING AND MERINGUE:
3 eggs, separated
1 (8-ounce) can sweetened condensed
    milk
1/2 cup fresh lemon juice
Grated zest of 1 lemon
6 tablespoons sugar

1. Preheat the oven to 350 degrees. Combine the graham cracker crumbs, 1 teaspoon sugar, and the melted butter. Press into a 9-inch pie plate. Chill 10 minutes.

2. To make the filling: In a bowl, beat the egg yolks with the condensed milk until well blended. Stir in the lemon juice and zest. Pour into the pie shell.

3. To make the meringue: In a bowl (not plastic), beat the egg whites until stiff. Gradually fold in 6 tablespoons sugar. Spread the meringue over the filling. Bake 15 minutes, or until the meringue is light golden brown. Chill well before serving, about 3 hours.

Holidays of Our Own
African-American Traditions

Dinner on the Grounds

Some of my mother's fondest memories are of the goodies contained in my grandmother Willie Mae's picnic basket when their Oklahoma church had its annual "dinner on the grounds." This dinner was usually held on Memorial Day. The pastor would offer up a prayer and then the men and boys would clean and weed the graves around the church while the women and girls set the long plank tables for dinner.

After the graves were clean, the women and children would decorate them with home-made crepe-paper flowers of brilliant hues. Some families would plant flowering bushes or trees near the headstones. Once the graveyard was perfectly tidy and beautifully decorated, it was time for dinner.

Each mother brought a sparkling-clean white sheet for a tablecloth. Then, as if by magic, the table would be covered with some of the finest food in Oklahoma! After an interval of concentrated eating, the families would move from table to table to sample Sister Davis's pie or Sister Caroline's potato salad. Each cook had at least one delicious specialty that was always in demand at church gatherings.

After dinner, the adults had a rare chance to visit, while the children played ring games, hide-and-go-seek, and stickball. Memorial Day is seldom celebrated in this manner anymore, although such observances should be revived. The foods traditionally served on the church grounds are easy to pack in modern picnic baskets. This menu includes some of those specialty dishes from long ago.

Angeline's Raisin-Pecan Pie

YIELD: 1 (9-INCH) PIE

1¹/2 cups raisins
1¹/4 cups sugar
8 tablespoons (1 stick) butter, softened
2 eggs
1 teaspoon ground nutmeg

1 teaspoon ground cinnamon
1 teaspoon vanilla extract
1 cup pecan halves
1 unbaked 9-inch pie shell (page 250)

1. Preheat the oven to 325 degrees. Put the raisins in a bowl of warm water to plump, 3 to 5 minutes. Drain, and set aside.

2. Cream the sugar and butter until fluffy. Stir in the eggs, one at a time, and combine well. Using a spoon, mix in the nutmeg, cinnamon, and vanilla. Scrape down the bowl. Fold in the raisins and pecans.

3. Scrape the mixture out of the bowl and into the unbaked pie shell. Bake until golden brown and set, 45 minutes to 1 hour, checking occasionally to make sure it doesn't overcook. If crust is browning too quickly, make a foil collar to protect it. The pie should be set, except for a soft center a little larger than a quarter. Remove the pie from the oven and allow it to cool 3 to 4 hours before serving.

Juneteenth

June 19 is the date of our emancipation celebration here in Texas. On June 19, 1865, Major General Gordon Granger stood on the balcony of Ashton Villa in Galveston and read an order from President Abraham Lincoln proclaiming that all slaves were now free. The newly liberated slaves reacted in different ways to Granger's news. Some fell on their knees in prayer. Others shouted and cried for joy. African-American Texans have celebrated June 19, or Juneteenth, for short, ever since.

President Lincoln signed the Emancipation Proclamation that freed the slaves on January 1, 1863. It seems hard to believe that it took two years and six months for the news to reach the slaves in Texas. A slave folktale says that President Lincoln sent the news from Washington by a Union soldier who rode all the way on a mule. Others believe that even though news did travel slowly, many slaveholders knew about the Emancipation Proclamation but refused to free their slaves. President Lincoln finally had to send Major General Granger and a squad of soldiers to free the two hundred thousand African-Americans who were still in slavery in Texas.

Juneteenth is celebrated in Texas in a variety of ways. In Austin, we have a parade, a beauty contest, handmade-craft booths, concerts, and of course food and lots of it.

Menu

Jerk Pork (page 89)
Pasta Vegetable Salad (page 258)
Fruit Salad (page 119)
Pickled Beets (page 222)
Red Rice (page 151)
Oven-Roasted Potatoes (page 240)
Toasted Butter Pecan Cake (page 247)

Pasta Vegetable Salad

YIELD: 6 SERVINGS

1 (12-ounce) can vegetable juice
1/4 cup finely chopped onion
3 tablespoons tarragon-flavored vinegar
2 tablespoons vegetable oil
1/2 teaspoon dried basil leaves, crushed
    between your fingers
1 teaspoon salt

1 teaspoon black pepper
1/2 teaspoon minced garlic
3 cups cooked drained rotini
2 cups broccoli florets
2 cups halved cherry tomatoes
1/2 cup sliced pitted black olives

1. In a jar with a screw-on top, combine the vegetable juice, onion, vinegar, oil, basil, salt, pepper, and garlic. Shake until thoroughly mixed. In a large bowl, combine the remaining ingredients. Pour the dressing over the pasta mixture and toss to coat. Cover and refrigerate at least 6 hours, tossing occasionally.

Christmas Gift!

Simon Brown was a slave on a Virginia plantation during the 1800s. His recollections are contained in a book titled *The Days When the Animals Talked*. In the book, he gives an account of a game called Christmas Gift. The game was played whenever two people met on Christmas morning. Instead of saying "Good morning," whoever said "Christmas gift" first got a present from the other.

The winner usually received a gift of nutmeg-flavored cookies called tea cakes, molasses taffy, sweet potato candy, popcorn, nuts, or a bottle of homemade syrup. Everyone all over Brown's plantation, both whites and blacks, surprised each other on Christmas Day with shouts of "Christmas gift!" This is a custom you may want to revive in your family. Make sure you have plenty of these traditional presents on hand just in case you aren't quick enough to shout "Christmas gift" first.

Molasses Taffy

YIELD: 10 SERVINGS

2 cups sorghum molasses
2 tablespoons butter, plus more for pan
   and hands
1 teaspoon vanilla extract

1. In a saucepan, boil the molasses until it hardens and leaves the sides of the pan. Remove from the heat, add the butter and vanilla, and stir just enough to mix. Pour into a well greased platter or shallow pan. Let stand until the candy begins to stiffen at the edges. To pull the taffy, butter your hands lightly. Take a fist-sized portion of taffy, pull it out, and fold it back repeatedly until the candy changes to a golden color, 5 to 10 minutes. When the taffy begins to harden, break it into sticks, tie it into knots, or twist it into rings.

Sweet Potato Candy

YIELD: ABOUT 36 PIECES

2 pounds sweet potatoes, peeled, boiled,
   and mashed
4 cups sugar
2 teaspoons fresh lemon juice

1 teaspoon pineapple juice, apple juice,
   orange juice, vanilla extract, or
   cinnamon, according to taste
Confectioners' sugar, for dusting the
   candies

1. Put the mashed sweet potatoes in a pan and add the sugar and lemon juice. Cook over low heat, stirring constantly, until the mixture separates easily from the pan. Set aside to cool completely. Add the flavoring. Take small portions of the mixture, dust in the confectioner's sugar, and roll out into 12-inch-long sticks. Set aside to dry. Wrap in wax-paper twists.

Kwanzaa

From December 26th until the new year begins, Kwanzaa is celebrated by many African-Americans. Kwanzaa was developed in 1966 by Dr. Maulana Ron Karenga, a professor of black studies at California State University in Long Beach. Dr. Karenga also established a special set of goals called the Nguzo Saba to be memorized, discussed, and acted upon during the seven days of Kwanzaa, and throughout the year. The Nguzo Saba means "seven principles" in Swahili. The first principle of Nguzo Saba is Umoja, or unity; the second is Kujichagulia, or self-determination; the third is Ujima, or collective work and responsibility; the fourth is Ujamaa, or cooperative economics; the fifth is Nia, or purpose; the sixth is Kuumba, or creativity; and the seventh is Imani, or faith.

Kwanzaa is neither a religious holiday nor one that honors a heroic person. Kwanzaa is a cultural holiday. This is a time when African-Americans join together to honor the heritage and traditions of their ancestors. Planning for the year to come, and working on ways to improve yourself and your community are important parts of the holiday. Kwanzaa is a celebration of the past, the present, and the future of African-American people.

One the sixth day of Kwanzaa, December 31, the Kwanzaa Karamu feast is held. During the Karamu Feast, family and friends gather together to celebrate our culture, our ancestors, and the community. The menu I've created for Kwanzaa includes some of the ingredients that Africans brought to America (black-eyed peas, okra, sesame, and peanuts), as well as recipes from the places where our ancestors were enslaved, to infuse the Kwanzaa celebration with the gifts of the ancestors and a taste of history. Enjoy and Harambee!

Menu

Ethiopian Party Punch (page 262)
Peanuts Piri-Piri (page 22)
Okra Salad (page 24)
Sesame Chicken (page 261)
Creole-Style Green Beans (page 98)
Mess of Greens (page 243)
Candied Yams (page 147)
Kuumba Pie (page 262)

Sesame Chicken

YIELD: 4 SERVINGS

2²/₃ cup evaporated milk

2 tablespoons plus 1 teaspoon
 Worcestershire sauce

1 teaspoon salt

1 teaspoon black pepper

1 teaspoon poultry seasoning

1 teaspoon garlic powder

¹/₈ teaspoon Tabasco sauce

1 (2¹/₂- to 3-pound) chicken, cut into
 8 pieces

2 cups panko bread crumbs

¹/₄ cup sesame seeds

2 tablespoons butter, melted

1. In a large bowl with a tight-fitting lid, combine evaporated milk with 2 tablespoons of the Worcestershire sauce, the salt, pepper, poultry seasoning, garlic powder, and Tabasco sauce. Mix well. Add the chicken, turning each piece to coat. Cover and refrigerate for at least 2 hours. Combine the bread crumbs with the sesame seeds. Roll the chicken in the crumb mixture until well coated.

2. Preheat the oven to 425 degrees. Put a sheet of foil paper on a rimmed cookie sheet and put the sheet pan in the oven to heat, about 10 minutes.

3. Remove the heated pan from the oven and place the chicken skin side up on the pan. Combine the melted butter with the remaining 1 teaspoon Worcestershire sauce. Drizzle the sauce over the chicken. Bake chicken 1 hour, or until done.

Ethiopian Party Punch

YIELD 12 SERVINGS

"Let your motto be resistance! Resistance! RESISTANCE! No oppressed people have ever secured their liberty without resistance." —Henry Highland Garnet

1 cup maraschino-cherry juice

1 cup strawberry syrup

1 cup orange juice

1 cup fresh lemon juice

1 cup pineapple juice

1 cup grape juice

2 1/2 quarts 7-Up

2 lemons, sliced thin

1. Mix all the ingredients except lemon slices together. Chill. Serve over ice. Garnish with lemon slices.

Kuumba Pie

YIELD: 8 SERVINGS

4 eggs

1 cup light corn syrup

2/3 cup sugar

3 tablespoons melted butter

1 tablespoon vanilla extract

1 tablespoon almond extract

1 tablespoon chocolate extract

6 ounces white chocolate, melted

1 cup pecan halves

1 cup slivered almonds

1 unbaked 9-inch pie shell (page TK)

1. Preheat the oven to 350 degrees. In a large bowl, using a mixer, beat the eggs until fluffy. Add the rest of the filling ingredients except for the pecans and almonds. Mix until well blended. Stir in the pecans and almonds. Pour the mixture into the pie shell. Bake for 50 to 55 minutes, until set.

Index